I0016236

Free Marketing
in Social Media

500 Tactics & Best Practices

Twitter, Facebook, MySpace, YouTube &More

By

Ronald D. Geskey, Sr.
2020:Marketing Communications LLC

"Marketing is no longer about the stuff you make, but the stories you tell."

--Seth Godin

2020:Marketing Communications LLC

Free Marketing in Social Media:

500 Tactics and Best Practices

ISBN: 978-0-557-23251-2

Copyright 2009 by Ronald D. Geskey, Sr.

2020:Marketing Communications LLC

Disclaimer

FREE MARKETING IN SOCIAL MEDIA

In Outer Space,

Can Anyone

Hear You Tweet?

Table of Contents

"Social media offer new opportunities
to activate...
brand enthusiasm."

--Stacy DeBuff, founder & CEO
Mom Central

Preface

In the "old days of the 1990s," marketing was a whole lot simpler. Clients worked with their agencies to develop big creative ideas that translated into memorable TV campaigns. Chevrolet, the Heartbeat of America; the Jolly Green Giant, Ho, Ho, Ho; Keebler Elves with secret flavor chips - you know what I mean. These campaigns were exposed to large audiences via mass media buys consisting of popular television programs, radio stations, magazines, and other mass media.

Even in the age of the proliferation of cable channels in the 1990s, media planning was simpler than today. Today, the rules have completely changed. TV advertising, while still very important is perceived by big advertisers as becoming less effective, efficient, and prominent.

Even within online budgets, consumer-generated media represents almost 20% of time spent but less than 3% of total dollars which underscores the labor intensity and cost efficiency of social media.

Engagement

Today, the most pressing marketing communications issue has shifted from clever ads and which media vehicles should be utilized... to trying to figure out how to best **engage** targeted consumers who might be interested in in a hopefully relevant message. In fact, the Advertising Research Foundation (ARF) is now promoting ***Engagement*** as the "new" model for how marketing communications should work.

Engaging consumers is what social media are all about. Imagine having a large group of consumers who follow you because they are actually interested in what you have to say. They are willing to enter into a dialogue with you. They will readily tell you what they like and don't like. And, as you will see, there are many types of social media available. Conceptually, using social media (intelligently) is almost a no brainer. But executing effectively is a challenge because the devil is in the details.

Web Site Traffic

Social media can help build traffic to your web site. Because social media can be so viral, it is possible to build high traffic to your web site. It's almost like multi-level marketing-- where one friend tells two others who tell two others who tell others – until, like the late Senator Everett Dirkson said about the government spending a billion dollars, "Pretty soon, you'll be talking about real money."

It's Free

To say the least, an extremely attractive benefit of marketing with social media is that it can be FREE or at least nearly free. You can register and begin building your presence for no money other than the cost of computers and time. Of course, you may decide to spend money to build your network or message, but even that is inexpensive compared to traditional media alternatives.

The Devil is in the Details

Social media are kind of complicated. There are different kinds of sites, zillions of applications different etiquette, the need for creativity and communication skills, and more. To be as successful as you can be, recognize that the devil is in the details. Obviously, the strategy behind using social media is important, but results will also be determined by how effectively each of the social media programs is *executed.* That's the reason for this book.

Purpose of this Book

Rarely have I made such a heretical statement, but "Marketing success in social media depends more upon execution than strategy."

The purpose of *Free Marketing with Social Media* is to provide a *primer* for marketers who are interested in (or are evaluating) the use of social media, but need executional ideas to make it work– i.e., *ideas for tactics and best practices.* This book will therefore provide 1) a strategic overview of social media and 2) a set of tactics and best practices which readers may follow once the decision has been made to execute a social media plan.

Free Marketing with Social Media provides an overview of social media marketing and explores nine of the most prominent social media in terms of marketing use - with heavy emphasis on tactics and best practices for executing effective and profitable programs.

As indicated, this book focuses on nine of the more important social media marketing opportunities: Twitter, Facebook, My Space, Digg, LinkedIn, Squidoo, StumbleUpon, Yahoo! Answers, and YouTube.

###

Chapter 1

Social Media in Marketing

Initially used as a way for family and friends to stay in touch and share, social media are now fast becoming an important marketing tool as well. A vast majority of Advertising Age or AdWeek issues devote significant space to various aspects of social media and marketing. Advertising agencies-- like Campbell Ewald-- are adding senior social media marketing specialists to their staffs. People in public relations monitor social media to identify any impending crises or trends in public opinion. Even small businesses are jumping aboard.

Social Media Defined

There are many different definitions of social media. Some are technology oriented, some rather confusing. Instead of referring back to the popular definition found on the likes of Wikipedia, a better definition, in my opinion, is one by Joseph Thornley, CEO of the PR firm Thornley Fallis. (Joseph Thornley, "What is Social Media?" 2008.)

"Social media are online communications in which individuals shift fluidly and flexibly between the role of audience and author. To do this, they use social software that enables anyone without knowledge of coding, to post, comment on, share or mash up content and to form communities around shared interests."

Another simple definition comes from Isabella Hilborn from her blog.

"Social Media. Any communications format where the users publish the content."

She continues, "Is that clear enough? Yes, it can be multimedia - music, pictures, video as well as text. Yes, it can be a blog or a social network like Facebook. Open Source is social media, although they would hate to be associated with a term that traditional marketers are trying to hijack. Social media can even be offline - like for girls, the citizens' band in radio, even the op-ed page of the New York Times (although arguably so because it is tightly controlled).

Hilborn adds, "Social media is media by society - as opposed to the top-down publishing model where one person (company, really) with a controlling editorial voice is in charge of the voice of the publication or the channel."

Therefore, social media are those in which the users create the content and are interactive, regardless of the communication platform.

Examples of Social Media

Some of the more popular social media applications are listed shown below.

- **Blogs.** Blogger, LiveJournal, Open Diary, TypePad, WordPress, Vox, ExpressionEngine, Xandi
- **Micro-blogging / Presence applications.** Twitter, Plurk, Tumblr, Jaiku, fmylife
- **Social networking.** Bebo, Facebook, LinkedIn, MySpace, Orkut, Skyrock, Hi5, Ning, Elgg
- **Social network aggregation.** NutshellMail, FriendFeed
- **Events.** Upcoming, Eventful, Meetup.com
- **Wikis.** Wikipedia, PBwiki, Wetpaint
- **Social bookmarking (or social tagging).** Delicious, StumbleUpon, Google Reader, CiteULike
- **Social news.** Digg, Mixx, Reddit, NowPublic
- **Opinion sites.** epinions, Yelp
- **Photo sharing.** Flickr, Zooomr, Photobucket, SmugMug, Picasa
- **Video sharing.** YouTube, Vimeo, sevenload
- **Livecasting.** Ustream.tv, Justin.tv, Stickam
- **Audio and Music Sharing.** imeem, The Hype Machine, Last.fm, ccMixter
- **Media & Entertainment Platforms.** Cisco Eos
- **Virtual worlds.** Second Life, The Sims Online, Forterra
- **Game sharing.** Miniclip, Kongregate

This book focuses on examples from different categories: Micro-blogging (Twitter), Social Networking (Facebook, LinkedIn, MySpace), Social Bookmarking (Stumble Upon), Social News (Digg), Video Sharing (YouTube), and others.

In recent years, numerous companies and brands have used these and many other platforms and channels to market their products.

Social Media in Marketing

As stated earlier, Social Media were used initially by individuals for personal purposes. They were a great vehicle for staying in touch with family and friends, networking, sharing information and opinions on blogs, posting photos,and more. Now, social media are also developing into an effective marketing tool.

Social media marketing is the process of promoting your products, site or business through social media channels. Social media are developing into a powerful marketing tool that will get you links, gain more exposure, draw attention, generate more traffic, and close more sales.

There is no other low-cost promotional method out there that is as effective in generating a large number of visitors, some of whom may become repeat visitors to your website.

Whether you are selling products/services or just publishing content for ad revenue, social media marketing is a potent method that will make your site profitable over time.

Role of Social Media in Marketing

While social media are obviously not the single panacea for marketing ailments social media can play an important role in the marketing communications mix for many companies, both in terms of branding and web site traffic.

Branding

The focus of advertising and marketing communications planning is currently shifting from passively "reaching" a target audience with a mass message (e.g., via a commercial within a television program or on a radio station) to ***engaging*** the consumer on a deeper level. The key to engagement is ***relevance*** of message and media to the audience.

The Advertising Research Foundation (ARF) defines engagement as the *"extent to which a consumer has a meaningful brand experience when exposed to commercial advertising, sponsorship, television contact, or other experience."*

Social media networking tools like Twitter and Facebook, if used intelligently and creatively, can be great tools for strengthening the relationship between a brand (advertiser) and the consumer. By definition, creating beneficial two-way communication between the marketer and the consumer should likely result in a stronger relationship.

In addition, social media can provide brands with valuable feedback on consumer/user likes and dislikes, preferences, suggestions, product opinion, and advertising issues. This kind of consumer feedback can help ensure that the marketer creates the right products at the right time to be in the right distribution channels at the right price and communicated in the right, effective manner.

As social networking tools like Twitter and Facebook continue to increase in popularity, and marketers figure out how to use these "new media," we will likely see marketing and media mixes including more social media. Facebook and others have already broken through some of the boundaries of conventional advertising. For example, Facebook is offering many, many new applications and tools which will help marketers.

Web Site Traffic

While web site traffic objectives are intertwined with branding objectives, social media can also help drive a large volume of targeted traffic to the advertiser's website. For example, as will be discussed later, to generate traffic to your website, you can join relevant groups, post relevant messages about your products or articles, aggressively develop your network, and more.

Furthermore and maybe best of all, the cost of this traffic is minimal because the initial out of pocket cost of social media is so low (primarily overhead, cost of computers, and time). Of course, if advertising is used, there is cost.

Benefits of Social Media/Marketing

What do leading marketers think the benefits of social media and marketing are?

A good place to start is with the 2008 research conducted by *eMarketer* among several hundred marketing executives. The purpose of the research was to identify marketing executives' perceptions of the benefits of social media marketing.

Findings

Following is a summary of the findings of the study:

1. ***Engagement*** – Perhaps not surprisingly, 85% believed that the main benefit of social media marketing was *customer engagement* -- which is consistent with the direction proposed by the Advertising Research Foundation (ARF).

2. ***Direct Consumer Communication*** – 65% said an important benefit is communicating directly with consumers- provides quick feedback which allows marketers to learn about and monitor consumer and customer preferences and issues in more real time and on a more regular basis.

3. ***Low Cost*** – 51% of marketers thought that low is an important benefit. Using social media is almost free (though pretty labor intensive to properly manage). Costs primarily consist of computer equipment, and staff, and any paid advertising you decide to buy on social media websites.

4. ***Brand Building.*** According to 48% of these marketers, brand building is one of the most important benefits. Why? Because engaging and building long term relationships with customers and potential customers helps to build brand equity.

5. ***Market Research–42% say Research.*** Having conversations with consumers and customers in social media provides an opportunity to collect and monitor consumer preferences and attitudes, competitive intelligence, and opinions on marketing tactics. In addition, social media can function as a kind of "early warning" system in the case of unforeseen issues – such as an issue in product quality. Monitoring the voice of the customer is one of the most important things a marketer can do and creating a solution that allows them to constantly give you feedback is usually a smart thing to invest in.

6. ***Reach*** - 37% say reach is most important. Planned and

executed properly, social media can target people who are most important to building brand sales. Social media also have the advantage of the multiplier effect – like multi-level marketing. Very large audiences are built through word of mouth - when people pass along information about the brand or website to another person. This extends the ability of social media to help generate leads and contribute to customer satisfaction.

Are Social Media Cost Effective?

Are social media cost effective compared to traditional media channels? The formula for cost effectiveness is:

Cost Effectiveness = Cost/Value Received

On the cost side of the equation, out of pocket dollars can be minimal, but your time spent can be great (which some would consider cost), plus advertising costs. So, for example, if you spent $1000 and received thousands conversations with consumers, received some good suggestions on your product and advertising, and generated a a few thousand visitors to your web site, is that cost effective compared to Google CPC or direct mail or whatever you use?

In addition to the perceived benefits of social marketing presented above, here are some additional "value" factors to consider in making a determination of value received.

1. *Viral Reach* - Given the potential multiplier (viral) effect, the number of "right people" you can potentially reach and/or bring to your website is huge... thousands or even

2. *.Millions* if your campaign is meaningful and well

12

executed. Given that the cost is zero or minimal, one would have to conclude that social media can be extremely cost effective. On the other hand, obviously, if you have a weak marketing concept and do not use results oriented tactics and best practices, your social marketing effort could be a waste of your time and whatever money you put into it.

3. ***Relating to Consumers*** - Using social media tools has become second nature to a large percentage of customers for many product and service categories (assuming they're familiar with the web). There is also a sense of consumer comfort with social media because people feel that they are free to say what they want without the fear of being gagged or ridiculed. Consumers tend to open up more and you will get a lot more honest feedback.

4. ***Continuity*** - Traditional media cannot be altered, while a social media platform is a living, dynamic, constantly evolving platform that allows you to connect with customers constantly. What is the value of continuity to you

5. ***Recency*** - One of the other major advantages is having the ability to send and receive messages and information almost instantly to users already tapped into the syste to youm.

6. ***Analytics.*** Modern social media platforms allow you to generate the kind of analytics you can only dream of in traditional media!

7. ***Cost Effectiveness.*** Because the cost of social media

8. programs is usually so low, it is quite cost effective - provided that the planning and execution are on target. Consequently, ROI should far exceed that obtained from traditional media channels.

Conclusion

Social media have come a long way, baby!

Because social media involve two way communications between marketers and consumers, social media offer an enhanced ability to engage and connect with consumers, concurrently providing valuable feedback to the marketers.

In addition, monitoring social media can be an *early warning system*-- enabling companies to tackle issues before they snowball into crises. Catching a product issue or an inadvertently offensive marketing tactic (when it's still in its early stage) is critical damage control compared to something spiraling out of control.

With this brief introduction to marketing with social media, the balance of the book will discuss some of the more popular social media applications, beginning with our first tweet on Twitter!

###

Chapter 2

Marketing with Twitter

*The first social media opportunity we will discuss is **Twitter** – which has been getting more than its fair share of press coverage in the past year. We will ask and answer several important questions: What is Twitter? What are its marketing applications? What are the tactics and best practices that should be considered by those using Twitter as a marketing vehicle?*

What is Twitter?

Twitter (www.Twitter.com), one of the top 50 sites in terms of worldwide Alexa traffic, was founded by Jack Dorsey, Biz Stone, and Evan Williams in March 2006 (launched publicly in July 2006). Twitter is a social networking and micro-blogging service that allows users to post their latest updates-- which are limited to

15

140 characters. The updates are called "tweets" and can be posted ₂₃in three ways:: web form, text message, or instant message. The company has been busy adding features to the product like G-Mail import and search. Twitter also recently launched a new section on its site called "Explore" for external and third party tools to interact with Twitter and a new visualization tool called Twitter Blocks.

Twitter as a Marketing Tool

For businesses/marketers, Twitter is another channel which connects and engages current and potential customers with your product or brand. It allows deeper infiltration into the values and lifestyles of interested participants, which should help build marketers build customer satisfaction and brand loyalty.

Kate Kay of ClickZ wrote about Twitter as a marketing tool in December 2008. "It's been called a tech-geek fad, a business flop-to-be, and waste of time for most marketers, she said, "but the fact is big name brands are on Twitter. While detractors argue brands don't even belong on the quick messaging platform, they are there -- from Ford to Dunkin' Donuts to Whole Foods. They're engaging in experiments with customer service, branding, and corporate culture-building in the decidedly public forum."

"Some see Twitter as an extension of the marketing department, she continues, "others view it as a customer service tool, and some say it's best for corporate communications."

Before joining Ford Motor Company in July as its global digital and multimedia communications manager, Scott Monty reportedly had a good following on his personal Tweeter account. "I wanted to get down and personal with people," said Monty, who believes Twitter enables that more so than Facebook, MySpace, or blogs. Getting personal made sense for Ford, which, according to Monty, hopes to "humanize the brand." (ClickZ)

Beyond branding, Twitter is also a **traffic generation tool**. The placement of links within profiles and conversations can direct visitors to specific website(s), and is "especially powerful if you are targeting early adopters and influencers."

As a lead acquisition tool, Twitter doesn't always reach the audience you want. Most Twitter users are somewhat web savvy, and it is sometimes difficult to target a specific subset of the general demographic and determine their level of potential interest

Twitter's Audience

What is Twitter's audience? Is it really a major factor in the media marketplace? As mentioned earlier, Twitter, according to a Wikipedia posting, is the 50th largest web sitge in the world as measured by Alexa.

Twitter's recent user growth has been nothing short of phenomenal. The rise of Twitter has been the talk of the tech and media worlds. In 2008, Twitter's users grew 422% and another 1,382% by early 2009.

By June 2009, according to internet audience research firm, *com.Score,* Twitter reached 44.5 million users worldwide, 20 million of whom are in the USA. So, Twitter's audience is larger than the audience for a decent prime time network TV program delivers.

According to Hitwise data, Twitter's demographic make up is quite different than that of Facebook or MSpace:

- 63% are males
- 26% are 35-44 years old
- 15% of Twitter visitors are "Stable Career" types, comprised of a "collection of young and ethnically diverse singles living in big-city metros like Los Angeles, Philadelphia and Miami." The Stable Career group tends to work in the arts and entertainment industry, drive small cars and espouse very liberal political views.
- 12% of Twitter's visitors are "Young Cosmopolitans," 40-somethings who are more likely to drive a Prius, earn household incomes over $250,000 per year and identify with very liberal politics.

Also, according to Hitwise, Twitter is no longer dominated by the 18-24 age group - middle aged men are now the key drivers! This may be in line with Twitter moving from being a *'my cat's been sick' status reporter*, to being used more widely as a distribution network and feed reader.

Steps to Using Twitter

Learning how to use Twitter is simple. So, let's start at the beginning, then move to some smart tactics and best practices. Here is what you have to do first to start Tweeting and growing your business.

1. ***Sign up for Twitter.*** As The first thing you have to do is sign up for free (at www.twitter.com). Twitter is a social networking site that is referred to as 'micro-blogging'. It involves the use of up-to-the-minute updates to share with

18

others what you are doing. Since Twitter is free, all you need to do is create an account to get started. Create a profile that outlines what you do. Include information relevant to your products that readers will find useful and interesting.

2. ***Follow Prospective Customers.*** A large Twitter following is a powerful way to increase website traffic with relatively little effort. Find like-minded people who may have an interest in your product or those that may have a problem your product can solve and start following them. People have the tendency to follow someone that follows them, so you the potential to quickly build a large following.

3. ***Update 'Tweets' Regularly.*** Update your micro-blog posts or 'tweets' on a regular basis to keep the content fresh. Tweets are limited to 140 characters, so keep it concise and to the point. Your tweets can include a link to your website along with a comment that may stir the interest of your potential customers. Use tweets to advertise specials and offer helpful tips relating to your products.

4. ***Post an Eye-Catching Picture.*** The image that you post on Twitter will be seen next to your tweets and will serve as an icon for your profile. It doesn't have to be a picture of you; it can be of your company logo, a product, or of any image to your liking.

5. ***Put Twitter on Your Website.*** Twitter offers badges that you can insert on your website so that your site visitors can see what you are doing and follow you on Twitter if they are not already doing so.

6. ***Keep Growing Your Following.*** Once you begin to create a

following on Twitter, you will watch it grow each day. The more people read your tweets, the more people will see your website link, and in turn you will start seeing an increase in website traffic at an unbelievable rate.

Follow these Twitter strategies to build a targeted audience following, keeping with the adage, "quality not quantity." You will be able to tell who the best tweeters are, the ones that get mentioned a lot, the ones that have spent some effort setting up their backgrounds, and add a lot of value. Next, we will get more specific with suggested tactics and best practices.

Tactics & Best Practices

Here are another 56 tactics and best practices to help you be successful using Twitter in your marketing plan.

1. *Use Twitter to Network* - With noteworthy business associates, competitors, and peers. You do not have to simply befriend every person that requests you or vice versa. Instead, choose your network carefully. Look for fellow executives or business owners who work within your particular niche.

   Then, follow their progress, look for advice, and of course, throw in some of your own ideas as well. Befriending people in the same line of work as you will give you an insider's look on how their successes compare to yours.

2. *Update your Audience Fairly Regularly* - But don't overload them. Most people will likely be interested in

3.   what you have to say, otherwise, they probably wouldn't have added you to begin with. With this in mind, you should update them on a fairly regular basis so they can keep abreast of what is happening in your world. On the other hand, you want to be sure not to over do it – which will give your audience the feeling that your Twitter site is "spammy," This is the quickest way to turn them away. Try to maintain a good balance and mix of meaningful, informative updates and other types of posts.

4.   ***Use Twitter Feed to Help People Stay Updated*** - Twitter feed is basically the website's answer to an RSS feed, and it is a great way to keep your followers updated without them manually checking your   page. It also allows things to be updated on their own, so you don't have to spend extra time telling everyone you have an update; it's all done for you.

5.   ***Use Twitter at Conferences and Trade Shows*** - When you're out and about networking in the REAL world, don't forget to use Twitter as an opportunity to update your customers and peers on what you're seeing and doing. This shows them that you're being proactive and it's a lot of fun as well.

You can tell them some funny things you may have come across at the trade show, or maybe inform them of an interesting vendor you've hooked up with. By sharing your experiences as you go along, you're generating more interest in what is happening with your business.

6.   ***Keep an Eye on What People are Saying*** - Don't forget, Twitter like any other virtual conversation is a two-way street. Pay attention to what other members are saying, and

21

see if they're Twittering about you. If they are, you may want to use that as an opportunity to either thank them for a nice compliment, or to make good if they are posting a complaint. Remember that you're never 100% immune from someone writing negatively about you, your website, or anything else on Twitter. Be sure to use this to your advantage and to be diplomatic.

7. ***Display your Twitter Profile*** - On business cards, your website, and in email signatures. Remind people in other ways that you're on Twitter. Some clients and customers might not know this until you directly pass the information along to them. Get a nice snapshot of your Twitter homepage and then display it along with a link to the page on your actual website. Include the page's URL in email signatures and you can even print this on a business card if you like.

8. ***Make Twitter Another Home Hub.*** Use Twitter to display your business growth, charts, statistics, and other factual data. This way, people who prefer to watch what's happening with you on Twitter have the same basic information and access as those who usually just visit your website.

9. ***Promote Events.*** Remember that the tool can be used for more than just updating people on the comings and goings of your business, but also to get them excited for upcoming events. This can be anything from an appearance at a trade show to a big seasonal sale or the launch of a new product. Always keep Twitter in mind when it comes to these updates and remember that it can reach a lot more people than just your email subscribers.

10. ***Filter your Traffic to other Places* -** You can use Twitter to also steer people to other resources that you use for marketing such as a blog page or website updates. The exchange of information through Twitter can go both ways, so keep that in mind. It's a good way to get others moving to different resources that you have available that they might not know about.

11. ***Find a Cool Template - That says who you are as company.*** Twitter now allows users to customize   the look of their home page. Make your Twitter page creative and unique. This can be the same graphics you use on your website or it can be your company logo or something you've customized just for Twitter. No matter what it is, make sure it's appealing to the eyes and does not look too "busy."

12. ***Why Email When you can Twitter?*** Don't send out short and sweet emails to your subscribers. Most people who opt in for company emails expect a monthly and at worst weekly update that is chock full of information. They don't want to open a short email with little to no valuable content. Save this for Twitter, where people hunger for the short sentences and blurbs. Then, you can compile all of these over the span of a month or so into one email for the others.

13. ***Use a Cool "Follow Me" Graphic.*** There are now hundreds of different "follow me" graphics to choose from that will grab people's attention. You can even customize your graphic if you want to, so people will see something distinctive about your page. Just like the template, the "follow me" graphics can get you noticed and trigger people's interest for more information, so make sure this

graphic is done well.

14. ***Keep it Casual.*** Remember that Twitter is a social site, so it's got more of a casual feel than some websites may. Make sure the posts are generally light, with a touch of humor otherwise you may lose your core audience. The purpose of following others on Twitter is so that it's entertaining. If your posts are too serious or heavy, it might turn some readers off.

15. ***Sub-Divide your Twitter Page -*** You don't have to have just ONE company page. Instead, try to come up with a page for all of your staff. This way, your customers get to know others on the team. It also adds a bit of diversity for the business, and gives people a cast of characters to follow instead of a faceless, nameless company. It also entices people to follow more so they stay connected to both you and your business.

16. ***Incorporate Video into your Twitter Page -*** Many people may not know, but Twitter allows for multimedia additions, so feel free to include video plug-ins on your page. This makes it more exciting, and people will want to follow your postings more closely if there are videos.

17. ***Divide and Conquer -*** You can parse your followers into different groups. This can actually prove to be quite useful, especially if there is a mix of followers that are customers, peers, competitors, and personal contacts. This way, you only update the people who care about certain things with particular tweets, while the others don't have to see those. It's a good way to hone in on your audience's interests.

18. ***Itunes, Iphones, and Twitter.*** There are a plethora of new

24

tools available that are incorporated into Apple's applications. This makes your Twitter updates available to busy people who are on the go, and for people who access your page solely on their Iphones.

19. ***It's not just for Iphones any More*** - Aside from Iphone specific applications, there are plenty of other mobile Twitter-related apps out there that you can use. Not only can your users download these apps and use them on their cell phones, but you can do the same and follow your friends and cohorts as well.

20. ***Inform your Customers of Stock Status*** - Twitter also has tons of great features and plug-ins that will notify your customers when certain items you carry are in stock and when they go on sale. This is an excellent way to notify people so they can make a purchase. This is also helpful for you, so you can get a jump start on your suppliers and what they are offering for you.

21. ***Map it Out*** - Google Maps and many other map sites now integrate with Twitter. This can be fun to show your followers where you're traveling, or even to simply show them where your business is located. It also comes in handy when you want to look up where your posters are located.

22. ***Digging for other Blogs through Twitter*** - Twitter is a great way to get some insight into other blogging websites such as Digg and other related sources. This can be a good way to not only find other peoples' blogs, but to link to them and inform other people about their content. By doing a search, you can find tons of great blogs on the web that can be linked to your Twitter.

25

23. ***Contests are Tons of Fun on Twitter*** - Host an impromptu giveaway contest on Twitter. You can do this every day, every week, monthly, whatever you choose. It's a great way to get all of your followers to stay interested and engaged, and freebies are always a guaranteed way of getting new contacts.

24. ***Ask for Feedback*** - Don't just tell everyone what you're doing via Twitter, try to ask everyone for their opinion and feedback. It's a good way to start a dialogue and to open up a forum for new suggestions and changes that can be made.

25. ***Colors Matter*** - Think about the color scheme of your Twitter page, and try to make it appealing and something that will fit your business' niche. For example, a NASCAR Twitter page wouldn't use a pink and red color scheme! Choose colors that fit your message and your style.

26. ***Type Fonts are Important, too*** - The fonts you use for the main Twitter page should also fit the theme of the business or page.

27. ***Make Twitter Followers Feel Special*** - By offering "Twitter followers only" Specials and Coupons. This encourages new purchases as well as new followers.

28. ***Offer More than just Twitter.*** If you're so inclined, let people know they can contact you outside of Twitter via email, text, or even phone. Open up various lines of communication.

29. ***Use Behind the Scenes Tools.*** Don't forget to look at metrics and what people click on and from where. This is definitely an invaluable tool.

30. *Get into a Routine.* Figure out a Twitter rhythm, and then stick with it. Once you get into the flow of posting, your readers will stick with you.

31. *Participate as Much as Possible.* Contribute, and be a part of others' Twitter pages as well. Don't just stand in the shadows or you might lose followers.

32. *Mix it Up.* Don't just use Twitter as a promotional site. Try to keep a dialogue going, let people know what's happening, and other things aside from your promotions.

33. *Partner Up.* It can never hurt to form a partnership with some of your fellow tweeters. Come up with a network within a network, and you'll be amazed at the results.

34. *Realize there are other Avenues, and then Expand on Them.* While Twitter is great, don't neglect your other social media sites, blogs, and your own website!

35. *Take out the Trash.* You can always "unfollow" people who are not posting positive comments, other companies that spam you, or "junk" Twitter friends. Don't be afraid to clean house every once in a while.

36. *Future Tweets Reap Sweet Treats -* You can now use tools that allow you to type up your tweets in advance so you can plan ahead and then they will post to your account when you're ready. A great time saver!

37. *Automated Tweets can help you Prioritize -* There are tools where you can select certain topics or sub-topics for notification, so that the topics that are important to you will

be delivered daily, or at a frequency you choose.

38. *Use the Advanced Search to your Benefit* - Twitter and other tools related to it have advanced search options, so you can really find that niche poster or specified topic that you're interested in.

39. *Use Links* - Never mention a resource without linking, if at all possible, this way people trust your opinions because they're backed   up with real links.

40. *Try not to Abbreviate Too Much* - While Twitter only allows 140 characters and that can be tough to express yourself, try to avoid too many abbreviations.

41. *Avoid Offending People by using Bad Language*. While this seems obvious, a lot of people get carried away on Twitter. As a business, you want avoid foul language.

42. *Be as Thorough as you Can.* Be thorough when explaining who you are, what your company does, and what you have to offer.

43. *Stay Away from Arguments if Possible*. Some people may get obnoxious or belligerent on Twitter. Try to avoid arguments by just ignoring them, otherwise you can dig your own hole and make yourself look bad.

44. *Don't be Boring.* Do not talk about what you had for breakfast or the weather. Keep your posts fresh, fun, and interesting.

45. *Counts don't Count* - Do not worry about how many followers you have. This can distract you from the quality

of your posts.

46. *Refuse Spammers* - Keep spammers and spam mailers out of your Twitter feed or else they can ruin your page.

47. *Ask and Ye Shall Receive* - Don't be afraid to ask others to re-tweet your tweets, or to link you to their blogs, etc. Most people will oblige if you just ask. [34]

48. *Open up to your Audience* - Try to loosen up and have your other Tweeters do the same by being   honest, intimate, and real with your readers. People will really enjoy the candid postings and stay enthralled.

49. *Offer Downloadable Material* - You can always offer a PDF download or other material on your Twitter page for people to look at and get more information.

50. *Use SEO to your Advantage* - Do not to forget to utilize important keywords in the Twitter posts.

51. *Do not Stop   Posting Abruptly* - If you have to go on vacation, make sure you have a fill in tweets to fill your post so your readers stay tuned.

52. *Headline Should "Shock"* - Twitter is actually just a blogging platform, just like standard blogs. You can still get RSS feeds, you can ping your tweets and go about nurturing your posts just as if you were using a blog for web marketing. You have to call attention to yourself, e.g, with fantastic headlines. At the same time, it is important to maintain the same etiquette with Twitter as you would with other content you post on the web.

Since Twitter posts are limited to just 140 characters you have *very little space to post something that will grab someone's attention.* In many ways, this is a test of how good your headline can be! Yes, there are URL shortening services to add some space, but the nature of Twitter is that you give people something that is 'buzz worthy', shocking, and, in general, something that adds high value to their time. People do not want a barrage of posts about offers, affiliate sales, and non-stop hassling to trigger them to take action.

52. ***Generate a Targeted Following*** - Assuming you have a effective "message" strategy, the next thing you have to do is create a relevant, targeted audience of "followers" if you will. To create a following, the first thing you can do is to use Twitter search. In Twitter search, you can find out what people are looking for or what their interests are and even their geographical location! So, right away you can choose to follow people who have a real interest in a particular topic that is in line with your product or services.

You can also use external Twitter tools, such as Twellow which is a directory of people's biography on Twitter. This, again, can help you target more specific people based on people's interests. There are hundreds of Twitter tools now, but these two will help you get started on the right foot.

53. ***Generally, if you Follow Someone, Experience says that 8 out of 10 of them will Follow you Back!*** ***Important:*** if you start posting attention grabbing, relevant and informative content, your followers will soon start re-tweeting your tweets. This is one of the viral effects of Twitter, and this will start getting you mentioned and respected as good tweeter.

30

54. ***Give Benefits to Your Followers* -** This is crucial! As suggested previously, Twitter is just like any other web page. You have to provide information that people will find interesting and valuable to them. One of the ways to do this is similar to the way you would approach your website content. Conduct a keyword research – it will tell you what people are looking for and then you can simply post an article on your blog and then tweet about that article to get   traffic to your post.

55. **Use Automated Twitter Tools -** Another way is one that is more   automated and uses other external Twitter tools. You can   actually use Google alerts and turn them into RRS feeds and run them through an application called Tweet Later. TweetLater can schedule your posts to Twitter in combination with an URL shortening service such as Tiny URL or bit.ly. In essence, this application grabs feeds from Google on a keyword or words you designate and it sends out posts to your Twitter account with a link to that content. This is a clever way to come up with some great content for your posts. This helps you engage your followers and because it is automated, it helps save time. This will allow you to simply add manual posts as needed. By syndicating your content much like people do on their blogs, you are creating news and content that people can enjoy!

56. ***How to Promote Using Twitter* -** So if you understood the previous points, you will realize that promoting using Twitter is all about giving out free, quality information first and then thinking money second. Generally, I would not recommend posting a promotion on Twitter until you have about   four weeks of posting quality content and/or until you have accrued 1,000-2,000 followers. Once you've a level of trust with your followers and they value your

31

opinions – they will be more willing to take action on your affiliate's promotion. It is recommended that you post a soft promo using good headlines that will spark curiosity and interest.

Sometimes, adding a bit of humor works as well.

###

Chapter 3
Marketing with Facebook

The second social media opportunity we will discuss is Facebook, currently the leader in social media networking sites. We will again ask and answer: "What is Facebook? What are its applications to marketing? What are some important tactics and best practices to follow when building a Facebook presence?"

What is Facebook?

Facebook is a *global social networking website* that is operated and privately owned by Facebook, Inc. Users can add friends and send them messages, and update their personal profiles to communicate with friends and colleagues. Plus, users can join Facebook networks organized by city, workplace, school, and region.

While a student at Harvard, Mark Zuckerberg founded Facebook with his college computer science buddies, Eduardo Saverin,

Dustin Moskovitz and Chris Hughes. Initially, The Facebook's membership included only Harvard students, but was eventually expanded to other Ivy League, schools and Stanford University. Later Facebook was opened up to any university student, then high school students, and, finally, to anyone aged 13 and over.

Facebook has met with some controversy. It was blocked intermittently in several countries-- including Syria, China, and Iran, although Iran later unblocked Facebook in 2009. Facebook has also been banned at many places of work to discourage employees from wasting time communicating back and forth with friends. Privacy has also been an issue, and it has been compromised several times. Facebook is also facing several lawsuits from a number of Zuckerberg's former classmates, who claim that Facebook had stolen their source code and other intellectual property.

Facebook as a Marketing Tool

From a marketing standpoint, Facebook represents a potentially powerful viral marketing opportunity for marketers aiming at either younger or older groups.

Facebook Users

A January 2009 *Compete.com* study ranked Facebook as the most used social network defined by worldwide monthly active users, thus overtaking MySpace. Facebook reportedly hit *300 million users worldwide* (reported September 2009), half of whom use every day.

- Potential Global Audience – 300 million users and growing

- Potential U.S. Audience – 150+ million
- Increasingly balanced demographics for a broad range of
- products and services
- Maximizing marketing impact with Facebook requires doing a lot of things right (see Tactics & Best Practices).

Facebook User Demographics

From a media standpoint, Facebook obviously represents a huge potential audience. The difference between the <u>how</u> audience is generated by a television program vs. Facebook is important to understanding the nature of social media. For example, the audience generated by a television program is accomplished from the top down-- by the corporation in its selection of program content, talent, time period, and so on. Facebook's audience, on the other hand, is generated by the users creating and sharing content.

The *demographics* of Facebook users still skew toward women (56%), 18-24 year olds of college age, but *most of the growth is among 35+ year old users*. For example, while 41% of users are 18-24, the growth rate among the 35-54 year old demo is growing fastest (September 2009. vs. six months prior) with a+276% user growth and 194% growth among the 55+ age group.

Viral Marketing

Facebook has a huge user audience with enormous viral marketing potential-- some have generated millions of web site visits! Viral marketing is basically "spreading the word" through others. For example, if you begin with 10 "friends" who each get an additional 10 friends to your web site, each of whom gets another 10 friends to your web site, it is possible to generate millions of visitors or customers.

Cost

In terms of costs, Facebook, by most any measure, would be extremely cheap. Primary costs involve computers, staff time, and any optional advertising or promotion done on Facebook or on other sites. This is not to say, however, that there isn't a lot of "sweat equity" involved in the "free" claim. Managing a significant social media program can be quite labor intensive.

Putting Facebook to Work

Facebook can be used to find new customers, stay in touch with existing customers, promote new products or services or to serve as a near perfect customer service medium. Facebook provides users access to many functions and applications.

- Creating profiles
- Adding people to the friends list
- Forming networks
- Forming Groups
- Messaging
- Chat (New)
- Sharing Photos and videos
- Sharing Events

Today thousands of business owners and professionals thrive online because they know the secrets of using Facebook, which offers unprecedented opportunities for the large corporations and the individual professional alike.

Tactics & Best Practices

In the last few years, Facebook has gone from a college photo-sharing site to a burgeoning business- networking platform for self-promotion, advertising and multimedia interaction. With new apps and add-ons, Facebook users can send each other a virtual drink, create and host events, advertise their businesses through social ads, and more. When Charlie Gibson hosted the debate for the 2008 presidential candidates along with Facebook, the little networking site became a powerhouse in the online-marketing community.

Here are some tips that will help you get involved in Facebook marketing and exploit Facebook to reach new customers, promote your business and drive traffic to your website.

Getting Started

If you are not already registered with Facebook, here is a summary of how to get started (www.facebook.com).

1. ***Create an Account -*** Let every one know you have an account. There is a widget to help you find current users in your own address book. Be sure to set it up complete, listing your profile and any pictures. Also in the information tab, you can include your business bio, websites, emails and other contact information. This is very important for those who would like to find you.

   Once you start connecting with your "friends," you will be able to notify them of any updated information. For example, if you have a new exhibit, product service, book etc, putting this information on our page will get this information out quickly and immediately. This is a great way to communicate.

2. ***Set up a "Museum" Photo Album -*** You can have a photo

37

album of your business or store, customers or any other items of interest. Now you can let people take a quick view of what you are offering at your store and on your floors. Also, you can take pictures of the groups and tag those who have a FB page. This will notify all of their friends that they are in a picture. When they click on the link or picture it will take them to your album and they will look around.

Also let your visitors know that you would like them to send photos of their visit, or them using your product, etc. You can create an album of visitor's pictures and put them in there for their network to review.

3. ***Send out Invites to your Upcoming Events*** - When you have a scheduled event or a repeating event you can invite your network to attend. Use the calendar section and the event section to post your upcoming events. Maybe it's a lecture of someone famous, or just a symposium on a new find, or just a half price day if you bring a friend. Anything that you want to put on the calendar and would invite people to, send it out. People can RSVP via Facebook as well to even give you a feel of visitors that my come.

4. ***Change your "What's on your Mind" Headline Often*** - This line is next to your page picture of you or your logo. When you change this it will again notify all your friends of this update. You could say something like "today will be busy because of the new King Tut exhibit. Better get here early." People may reply or comment on this and again it just another way to keep in touch with your network. Also work to become a resource for the network. If you have an exhibit dealing with something you know they are studying in history at the local schools, spend a little bit of time adding content to your page via a blog or posting or note

this would give people a reason to go to our page which could lead them to your main website. BE CREATIVE.

5. ***Put it in your Advertising*** - Let your membership, visitors, etc., know that you have a Facebook page and ask them to add you as a friend.

    This is the quickest way to get your network numbers up so you can become a resource for them. Ask them to write comments about their trip or visit. You can approve what gets posted. Then once they are your friends, then you can go to their friends list and request that you be added as a friend. When they look to see who you are, it will show that you both have a friend in common. Once they see this it is no longer a "cold call" it is now a referral from a friend. They will be more likely to add you.

6. ***Create Fans*** - One way is to get a "fan," is to ask your friends to add you as a fan. When they do, it will be posted on their page. Their friends will check that list and might decide to become a fan of you as well. You can also communicate directly with your Fans. Do you see where this could be a great tool?

Marketing with Facebook - More Tips

Using Facebook as a professional marketing tool is a lot different than using it for enhancing one's social life. If you're planning to use Facebook platform for professional networking, we suggest that you follow the seven steps outlined below to separate your Facebook social life from your work life.

1. ***Create a <u>Professional Profile</u>*** - This is your second

resume. Use resume writing techniques to polish up your existing Facebook profile. List your expertise and accomplishments in the "Write something about yourself" section. Un-check everything in the "Looking for" section except Networking.

2. *Use Business Related Information* - In the Personal Information section, include the business book that you have recently read, some quotes from top business leaders in your field, your favorite business related TV show, and business magazines that you frequently read.

3. *Focus on Accomplishments* - In the **About Me** sub-section of the Personal Information section, elaborate on your past achievements and list skills that you used in the past to solve business problems.

4. *Look Grown Up* - Remove all beer drinking pictures with your college buddies and not-yet-an-adult applications from your profile. If you were a speaker in a seminar and you have pictures, upload them to your profile. If you have pictures with business leaders or intellects in your professional field use those pictures instead of your spring break surfing pictures, unless you are looking for networking with surfing professionals.

5. *Maintain Separate Social and Business Profiles* - If you want to keep your Facebook social life, create a second profile for your work life. People who are migrating from college life to a professional career will find it beneficial to keep the two profiles separate so that they can poke their college buddies and make business deals at the same time using the Facebook platform.

6. ***Start Reading and Publishing Content -*** Start posting content related to your industry. Publish content in various online magazines and post links to interesting and informative online content and tools in Facebook status. If you have a blog, publish your blog RSS field in Facebook's "My Notes."

7. ***Leverage Friends.*** Select a few dozen friends and keep in contact with them using Facebook email and chat. Check out the Facebook group they subscribe to and join those groups. Post thought provoking comments in those groups to make yourself more visible. Help others by offering solutions to their problems.

The important thing to keep in mind is that whatever you share in your Facebook account is visible to everybody in your network. So be careful about the image you project to the world!

While there are dedicated professional networking sites like LinkedIn, you can also use Facebook for establishing professional relationships and conducting business deals as well.

8. ***Put Together a Killer Profile page. -*** Create a profile page that will be informative and look attractive to your customers or business contacts. It doesn't necessarily have to be professionally designed, but it should be simple and effective. You should provide enough information to pique the interest of your target market.

9. ***Add your Business Contacts -*** Many business owners, professionals and entrepreneurs already have a Facebook account. Invite your business contacts and customers to

add you as their "friend" and invite those who do not have an account yet to get their own. This way, you can build a Facebook community around your business.

10. ***Network Around*** - Another great way to create a Facebook network around your company is to use the site's Groups feature to network with your business contacts. This feature also allows you to reach your target market as you join existing groups or create one just for your business.

11. ***Buy Ad Space.*** This requires a small investment, but it is still a lot more affordable than traditional advertising methods. Facebook provides you with the tools to create your ad and target it to a specific age group, gender and location. It even gives you the choice to pay per click (CPC) or impression (CPM). Finally, you have the ability to track your ad's performance.

12. ***Post in the Facebook Marketplace.*** You can promote and sell your products in the Facebook Marketplace for free. There are 130 million active users, a number that is still growing rapidly.

13. ***Promote your Blog.*** If you have a personal company or business blog, you can easily import it into your Facebook notes. Each of your blog postings will then appear in your news feed and that of your contacts. This is a fantastic way to keep your business contacts up-to-date with your blog.

14. ***Advertise an Event***. Facebook has developed a free application called *Facebook Events*, which allows you to promote meetings, conferences, marketing events you may be hosting, product launches and your company's achievements.

15. ***Sponsored Groups.*** Sponsor your own group on Facebook by purchasing a link that hosts ad content, message boards and more.

16. ***Mini-Feed.*** When it first came out, members weren't sure if they wanted to be updated each time a friend added new photos, changed their status or even wrote on someone else's Wall. As an advertiser, though, you can track your Mini-Feed to find out what your friends have been up to and more closely study your target audience.

17. ***AceBucks.*** Facebook users earn AceBucks by playing games and taking surveys, then cashing them in for real-life prizes like Wii systems and iPods. Create your own survey or game to promote your business and then invite others to play.

18. ***Business Opportunities on Facebook*** - Mashable! lists several moneymaking strategies available on Facebook, advertising and otherwise. These include selling applications, developing applications for third parties, advertising, selling services within Facebook.

19. ***Facebook's "Secret" Rate Card*** - While Facebook has historically denied having a rate card, they reportedly do have one focused on selling integrated advertising and promotion opportunities. Getting a hold of one may help you negotiate a better deal.

20. ***Promote your Cause via Facebook*** – If you are involved in cause marketing, TechSoup ("the technology place for non profits") shows nonprofits how to use Facebook for self-promotion.

21. ***Facebook Ads*** - Facebook's official advertising page strives to prove how social ads, profile pages and paid ads can increase a company's business.

22. ***Social Ads*** - Social Ads replaced Facebook Flyers in November 2007-- at the same time Facebook launched Pages. Ads may be text or image. With Social Ads, Facebook offers advertisers the option to pay on a CPC or CPM basis, whichever they prefer. Social Ads offer very powerful targeting capabilities. when you create your ad, you have the option to limit who sees your ad by age, sex, location, keywords, education level, workplaces, political views, and relationship status. They can be used to advertise your own web page or some content in Facebook. Social Ads are completely self-serve and provides real time feedback on the size of your target audience and the suggested bid range to achieve impressions. While Facebook doesn't guarantee your budget will be reached, it is unlikely that they're close to filling their inventory.

   Social Ads also offer placements in the News Feed which gets much better click through. You can also target Social Ads to friends of users who have recently engaged with your brand via your Facebook Page or Facebook Beacon (for more details on Beacon, see below). These units convert at a much better rate.

23. ***Profile Page.*** All Facebook members get their own profile page when they sign up. Use this as your canvas to upload pictures, logos and other information about your company.

24. ***Groups.*** Use the site's Groups feature to network with your target audience. You can join existing groups or create one

just for your business to amp up the buzz about its services.

25. *Facebook Marketplace.* College kids use the site's Marketplace to scout out used couches and find roommates, but a savvy business owner can advertise services and product sales, as well as search for new employees

26. *Networks.* Ignoring the Networks question when you create your company's profile could lose it a lot of business. List your business's city, industry, neighborhood and any other relevant information to let potential customers and business partners know where they can find you.

27. *Facebook Badge.* Facebook describes its Badge feature as "a customizable way to share your Facebook information on other Web sites." Creating your own Badge will link Facebook friends to your company's Web site.

28. *Events -* Instead of printing out flyers and mailers the next time you want to advertise an event, use the free Facebook Events app to get the word out.

29. *FunWall -* Mass emails are so yesteryear. If you want to keep in close contact with your Facebook friends, use the FunWall to create a message or send a greeting to everyone at once.

30. *Top Friends Network -* Reward your top friends by sending them a virtual drink or writing on their FunWalls. As a marketing tool, the Top Friends network serves as another way to group your contacts, keep an eye on your target demographic, and quickly and effectively reach out to your company's best customers.

31. ***Inbox*** - Send secure, private messages to your clients on Facebook with the Inbox app. You can still send out mass messages, but only to the contacts you select.

32. ***Notes*** - Mashable! calls Facebook's Notes application a blogging feature because of the way users post links, messages, photos and other information that they want to share with friends. Even if you maintain a blog elsewhere, give your Facebook friends an exclusive peek into your company's news and behind-the-scenes schedule by posting here.

33. ***Contact Importer.*** The contact importer helps you "find your friends on Facebook." If you want to find out if your clients or other work-related contacts use Facebook but think it's a little lame to come right out and ask, upload your contacts from AIM, Gmail, Outlook, Apple Mail and more to find out if they're online.

34. ***Share partners.*** When you publish updates to your company blog or Web site, add the link or a link and a photo to your Facebook profile using the Share Partners app.

35. ***Facebook Pages.*** A more business-savvy name for Profile, the Facebook Page now includes all kinds of add-ons so that you can post videos, logos, pictures and other marketing info.

36. ***Facebook Polls.*** Businesses can effectively find out what their target audiences are thinking by utilizing this polling service on Facebook.

37. ***Facebook Beacon.*** Connect your company's website to

your customers' Facebook profiles with the Beacon action alerts. By integrating just three lines of code, your customers can choose to let their friends see what they viewed and bought on your company's Web site and more.

38. ***Facebook Insights.*** Through charts and mapping devices, companies can accurately track their "presence and promotion on Facebook."

39. ***Facebook Platform.*** If you want stand out from the thousands of other Facebook advertisers, create your own tools and applications with Platform. This system helps Facebook users design interactive apps so that visitors and friends can easily explore what your company has to offer.

40. ***FeedBurner*** - Advertise your company's blog or podcast with the FeedBurner app for Facebook. A feed will appear on your profile, so visitors to your page are instantly updated with new postings, videos and more.

41. ***Gydget*** - Small companies, bands, nonprofit groups and other organizations should try out Gydget, "a stand-alone viral-promotions tool" that you can add to your Facebook page and also encourage others to integrate with their own pages Update fans and clients with details about upcoming events, networking opportunities, sales and product intros

42. ***Ether*** - Charge by the phone call when you list your Ether number on Facebook with this ingenious app. By adding the button to your Facebook page, you can advertise your expertise and invite friends to call you for advice.

43. ***Jobster*** - Attract new talent from the Facebook pool by integrating a Jobster button with your profile. Your

company can build its own job network, submit a listing in the Jobster network and more

44. *QOOP* - QOOP helps you create promotional items like T-shirts and mugs from digital photos. Facebook users can use the QOOP app to share the items by letting friends view and purchase your marketing creations.

45. *Oodle Classifieds* - Organize your company's advertisements, job postings and classifieds on Facebook with the Oodle app.

46. *Going Viral* - Going viral is one of the big advantages of social media. Following are some ideas recommended by some experts.

47. *Forced Invitations* - What exactly is this method you ask? As soon as someone decides to add your application they are required to invite 10 friends. It is a brute force method that can be used by those with popular applications that don't have rich feature sets. The point is to find ways to get others to multiply your friends.

48. *Invite After Action* - When the Facebook platform first launched there were no restrictions as to how many people an application user could invite per day. As a result many of the initial applications that took advantage of the check box invite forms grew rapidly. Since the launch, there is now a limit of 10 friends per day by each application user. While it has been significantly limited by Facebook, it is still a useful form of marketing. When building your application you should definitely come up with an effective way of allowing users to invite other people.

49. ***News Feed*** - *The news feed is the most powerful component of Facebook. Period.* There are two ways that applications can leverage the news feed. The first is naturally built in. Most of the time, when a user adds an application it is displayed in their friends' news feeds. While it is not a guarantee that it will show up in other people's news feeds (due to a number of factors pertaining to news feed optimization), this is the primary thing that helps applications spread virally. The second way of using a news feed is by leveraging the news feed API calls that Facebook provides. Within reason, you can regularly post news items to a user's mini-feed within their profile. A small percentage of the time that item will end up on their friends' news feeds. While this is severely limited, at least you can get it on to your users' mini-feeds. You should strive for every form of exposure you can get (within reason) for your application.

50. ***Referrals/Giveaways*** - This is the most recent form of viral marketing on Facebook. The referrals tactic is to come up with an effective way of encouraging your applications users to market your application for you. They can market it on blogs, websites, forums, Facebook walls, and messages to friends and more. The bottom line is that you end up with your users being the ones that get scrappy with the marketing, not you. Giveaways are usually combined with this to provide an incentive for users to promote your application. There is a potential risk, however, that it can make your application look cheap, but for now I think this is a great technique.

51. ***One-on-One*** - Used alone, this technique may not result in viral growth of your application, but combining this technique with one of the others previously mentioned can

lead to exceptional results. The concept is straight forward. Reach out to people that you think will find your application useful. This technique is more for targeted applications, not for generic ones such as poke wars, zombie biting, etc. Reach out to these individuals and then follow-up with them once they've added it. The result is that you will have passionate users that become your own brand evangelists. This technique has been used by countless communities to help generate passionate users. If you nurture your application users you will see positive results in the long-term.

###

Chapter 4
Marketing with MySpace

The third social media opportunity we will discuss is MySpace-- which has similarities and differences to other social networking competitors such as Facebook. We will discuss what MySpace is, what its marketing applications are, and what some important marketing best practices for those using MySpace.

What is MySpace?

Like Facebook, MySpace is a social networking website. Its headquarters is in Beverly Hills, California, where it shares an office building with its current owner, Fox Interactive Media (owned by News Corporation). MySpace became the most popular social networking site in the United States by June 2006, but by April 2009, according to *com.score*, MySpace was overtaken internationally by its main competitor, Facebook, in terms of monthly website visitors.

MySpace vs. Facebook

FREE MARKETING WITH SOCIAL MEDIA

There seems to be some confusion about whether MySpace is basically just another Facebook. Although there are some similarities, in actuality, these sites look and function quite differently. It is important that anyone looking to utilize these tools is aware of the differentiating aspects of the sites..

So what are the differences?

1. ***Profile Presentations*** - First, MySpace profiles are all unique; users can incorporate a variety of colors, photos and flash applications to their pages. On the other hand, Facebook's profiles are clean and uniform because Facebook uses a template design that cannot be modified (as it can be in MySpace).

2. ***Audience Differences*** – MySpace is popular with both the high school and young adult age groups as well as with the over 40 group-- with an average user age of 35. *Quantcast* reports (10/09) that 57% of MySpace users (in the U.S.) are female, 26% are teens, 46% are 18-34, and 26% are over 35. MySpace users tend to be below average in income and college education.

3. ***Site Etiquette is Different*** - On MySpace it is more socially acceptable to "friend request" or message random people. On Facebook that almost never happens, and it is considered border-line offensive. Facebook friends are generally people you actually know.

4. ***Functionality*** - Once you have figured out all of the basics, you can begin to familiarizing yourself with the really important differences — in functionality. Both sites have different applications and capabilities that make them unique and the more you know about them, the better you

can think creatively about how to apply them to your particular client or business.

MySpace's three unique functions are the ***bulletin board, blog posts and music applications.***

5. ***Profile Presentations -*** First, MySpace profiles are all unique; users can incorporate a variety of colors, photos and flash applications to their pages. On the other hand, Facebook's profiles are clean and uniform because Facebook uses a template design that cannot be modified (as it can be in MySpace).

6. ***Audience Differences*** – MySpace is popular with both the high school and young adult age groups as well as with the over 40 group-- with an average user age of 35. *Quantcast* reports (10/09) that 57% of MySpace users (in the U.S.) are female, 26% are teens, 46% are 18-34, and 26% are over 35. MySpace users tend to be below average in income and college education.

7. ***Bulletin Board -*** The first, the ***bulletin board,*** allows users to post messages which all of their "friends" will see upon login. Because of its visibility on the homepage, it is a quick and easy way to send messages to all of your friends at the same time.
8. ***Blog Area*** --The second, the ***blog area,*** appears on each profile and allows users to make blog posts without actually hosting a blog.

9. Music – And finally, MySpace's most effective function is the ability to ***add music to your profile***. This is a great way for musicians to get people to listen, share and download their music. It's one of MySpace's strengths and why the social network has become so famous for and effective in discovering new bands and new talent.

On the other hand, Facebook's applications are a phenomenon that have taken on a life of their own ever since its introduction. *Facebook now has many more applications than MySpace.* But the key is to be aware of the tools you have and to recognize that these sites are more than just a profile with your picture and some basic info. In the end, the more you know about the apps from both MySpace and Facebook, the smarter you can use them.

MySpace as a Marketing Tool

While declining, MySpace remains a very important marketing tool for certain marketers, especially if used in combination with Facebook.

Audience

MySpace has about 100-125 million total users world wide and 75 million in the U.S. The number of MySpace users has declined somewhat with the growing popularity of Facebook.

Monthly users are estimated to have declined from about 65-66 million U.S. users in April 2009 to approximately million monthly users in September 2009.

Demographics

Demographically, MySpace users are more likely to be female, and are still quite young (26% 13-17 and 46% 18-34). Users are also more likely to belong to an ethnic group, especially Hispanic. Because of their ages, no doubt, they are below average in income and college education. (Source: Quantcast)

Potential Marketing Application

MySpace can create an additional presence on the web especially for marketers who cater to MySpace's largely younger audience. Since MySpace is affiliated with MSN, anyone who uses Windows Live is more likely to find your "space." Increase website traffic with MySpace by networking with people who have similar interests (i.e. have the problem that your product can solve) and provide a link to your website on your space.

Reflecting back on the demographics of MySpace users, the network might be most relevant for products and services consumed by young consumers, particularly teens and the 18-34 group. On the other hand, some bloggers voice the more enthusiastic view of MySpace as represented below:

"MySpace is not only for teenagers and musicians. MySpace is also making a buzz among Internet marketers. At the invitation of Internet marketing guru Marlon Sanders, I set up a profile to see what the buzz is all about. Marlon calls it "...a 'secret' networking method the people on the inside are using."

Being the active experimenter that I am, once I got started, I couldn't stay away from MySpace, setting up my profile, posting on my blog, adding events to public calendar. As I poked around, I thought about how this networking space could work for professionals as a business tool.

It's pretty easy to set up a profile and it's free. If you're using it as a business tool, be professional about the information you reveal.

Remember MySpace is ultimately a SOCIAL tool and many people use it to hook up for dates and relationships. If that's not your intent, keep your content business-oriented.

What I noticed in looking at random profiles is that most are sloppy and incomplete. A lot have no information about the person and no photo. What's the point? My sense is that a lot of profiles get set up and then abandoned, much like blogs.

Tactics & Best Practices

Following are some tactics and best practices which should help you successfully and effectively execute a program on MySpace.

1. ***Should I Use a MySpace Service?*** There are a number of companies that offer services for MySpace marketing. The services that they offer are basically include creating a profile for you and adding a few thousand friends for you. You can buy these profiles ready-made right off these companies and then customize your URL. Some of these companies, on the ther hand, take your existing profile and add friends for you. They probably search for these friends through the market, interest or keyword that you specify. They help you build a profile without you really going out and adding friends by yourself, which I figure would take a really long time to add... lets say 2,000 friends.

2. ***Is it Worth it to Hire Someone to Build a Profile*** before you actively market your business on MySpace.com? Since MySpace offers some creative flexibility, a professional profile builder may be worth the cost. However, it also depends on how much money you want to spend. The great

56

thing about MySpace is that you can do it all for free if you want. Anyone who is actively involved in Internet marketing and doesn't have the time to spend, should seek creative services which can enhance your probability of success.

3. ***Should You Use a Friend Adder Program?*** You can also hire a company to find friends for you. The going rate for a 1,000-friend profile is about $10 - $15, which is really cheap. With a thousand friends you can get a lot of people to your website if you continue to send out bulletins or comments on their profiles.

It's really up to the person or the individual. There are a lot of "friend-adder" programs which could easily add a thousand friends in a short time. Add up to 300 friends a day if possible, but be sure you don't go over that because MySpace could delete your account if you go over that number! In addition, you probably want to keep your primary profile live just to target just your friends and acquaintances. You don't really want to use your primary profile for the purpose of marketing a product or offer.

4. ***Use Separate Profiles*** - It's better to use separate profiles dealing with different business segments which are surrounded by all your keywords and content that's geared towards the topic that you're trying to market. You really want to keep that separate from your primary profile.

5. ***Appropriate Products on MySpace*** - You need to be careful about what you market. MySpace is for the most part a younger crowd so you want to be careful of anything obscene. Any kind of money-making scheme or something that could be deemed illegal by MySpace would probably

put some scrutiny on your profile and get you deleted, so you want to stay away from that.

6. ***Max 300 Friends per Day*** - Be Careful when you're using a friend-adder program. As mentioned previously, if you go over 300 friends a day you can get your account deleted.

7. ***Start a MySpace Group*** - Build up your profile by starting a MySpace Group. Try to get everyone going with comments and once they do that it kind of takes off on its own. It really has that viral effect.

8. ***Generate Web Site Traffic*** - If you really have a good offer and headline in your profile you'll be amazed by how many people end up going to your website. You just need to make that offer compelling enough. You want o come right off and make it clear what is it that you want them to do by making the link pretty obvious, but you don't want to be "salesy" at all because the people in MySpace really turn away from that. So just give them as much information as possible, befriend them and you'll be rally shocked at how easy it is to do really well in MySpace. **Acquire lots of "Friends" on MySpace** - "Friends" are what drive MySpace.com. The more friends you have, the more popular your MySpace. This popularity is not about vanity. It's about viral marketing. *one click away.*

9. ***Be Very Cautious with Minors*** - Becoming Friends with prospective students aged 17 and under is where the MySpace etiquette comes in. MySpace has a safety feature where users can not "Search" for those aged 17 and under. There are creative ways of getting access to these users, but we don't suggest approaching these users with "Friend

58

Requests." First, they are minors and most likely an adult will be maintaining your MySpace profile. With the media's coverage of sexual predators on MySpace, it's just better to not proactively seek these users as Friends on MySpace. Second, these users don't like to be sought out or marketed to on MySpace. They find it intrusive and you run the risk, quite frankly, of annoying them. You're Friend request can easily be interpreted as spam. This age is particularly tech-savvy and territorial about their MySpace social networking,is extremely sensitive to spamming on MySpace.

10. Befriend States, Cities, Businesses, Non Profits - States, cities, businesses and nonprofit organizations Every state in the United States has a MySpace now – contact them and ask them to be friends and ask if they'd feature you in their top friends. Most large metropolitan areas also have a MySpace - contact them and ask them to be friends and if they'd feature you in their top friends. Businesses and nonprofit organizations are also jumping onto MySpace. If you have a partnership with any of these business or nonprofit organizations, become Friends.

11. Post "Comments." - This is a feature in MySpace that allows you to post "Comments" on your Friend's MySpace. The more Comments you post throughout MySpace, the more visibility your college or university's profile will have. This is a time-consuming process, so at Drury University we've limited our comments to "Happy Birthday" comments. As mentioned earlier, MySpace is driven by HTML, so we designed a very simple "Happy Birthday" graphic that we post when it's the birthday of one of friends. MySpace makes it easy for users to know when your Friend's birthdays are.

59

12. Posting "Bulletins" on MySpace - This is the most productive   feature on MySpace to engage your Friends. By default, your MySpace creates its own bulletin board visible to only to your Friends. Posting bulletins about upcoming events, polls or issues related to student/alumni life prompts your Friends to participate in your MySpace. One of the best practices is to integrate your bulletins with your blog entries. Using html, drive your Friends directly to your blog entries. Not only will they then be reminded to visit your MySpace and see what updates have been added since their last visit, but they are also prompted to comment on your blog. Send no more than 1-2 bulletins per day, and if possible, spread them out between mornings and afternoons. If you become "bulletin happy" you run the possibility of annoying your Friends and enacting the law of diminishing returns.

13. Blogging on MySpace - Each MySpace has their own blog with the top 5 blog entries being visible on your MySpace homepage. Again, these blog entries should not be focused on information, but rather interactivity. Users don't go to blogs to read and acquire information. They go to blogs to post "Blog Comments" and "Give Kudos." Of course, providing some information is required, but it should be short and users should be able the skim the information and it should be the sort of information that entices users to comment of give kudos. Here are some examples of successful blogs.

ATTN Alumni. What year did you graduate and what are you doing now?

POLL. Are you going to graduate school?

GO GREEK! Rush Week next week

Check out our new Environmental Studies program!

If you want to provide more information, you can link to the appropriate section/page on your university website. Mostly, the best practice in using blogs on MySpace is to ask a question that prompts users to respond.

14. *Events Calendars & Event Invitations.* MySpace has an excellent online calendar system. Post concerts, speaking engagements, prospective students events, theatre productions, rush week, athletic events, etc. Not only will these events reach prospective students, current students, alumni, but also members of your local community who are on MySpace.

15. *Become "Friends" with pop culture.* Every major, minor and up-and-coming musician and band in the United States –   increasing around the world – has a MySpace. You want   U2, The Fray, Hawthorne Heights, etc. to be your friend. First, having famous Friends brings an element of   "cool" to your MySpace. Second, you provide you Friends the opportunity to listen to this artist's music for free.

16. *Pop Culture* - MySpace also has a "Film" section. Movies marketed to teens and those in their 20's and 30's aren't even creating websites to market their films anymore – they are using MySpace. Becoming Friends with these films   give your MySpace provides the impression that you are hip to modern   pop culture. MySpace is constantly evolving definitely on the pulse of pop culture. You should be too. This is simple idea that can be blogged, commented and bulletined.

17. *Change your "Top Friends" on a monthly basis.* Users love being top friends on your MySpace. It gives them the feeling of being famous. The maximum number of top friends you can select at any given time is 24. After you have elected new Top Friends, post a comment on their MySpace letting them and their Friends know that they have made a top friend. You will definitely earn their loyalty with this simple MySpace best practice.

18. *Funnel your MySpace visitors to join your e-mail marketing and newsletter campaigns.* This is especially true of prospective students and alumni. Most likely your college or university spends thousands of dollars acquiring the e-mail addresses of prospective students and struggles to get the e-mail addresses of your alumni. They will be visiting your MySpace, so provide them the opportunity to "Subscribe" to your e-mail marketing e-newsletters.

19. *Use your "About Me" Section* - To talk about your business, products and services.   Make sure you have active hyperlinks that lead to your primary website, blog and products. It's a good idea to have a basic knowledge of HTML so you can add images and clickable links.

20. *Use the Blog Module* - Write about your business and events.

21. *Send "Bulletins" through the MySpace System* - To all your "friends" about your product launches, press releases, events, etc.

22. Join MySpace Groups - That represent your target audience. Participate in discussions and send bulletins to everyone in the group. No spamming!

23. Post your Events - On the public calendar.

24. Don't ever Spam your Friends Lists - Remember that commercial uses of MySpace are not encouraged; however, they may be tolerated, provided that your efforts are not overt and disruptive. For this reason, you will want to remain low-key. Avoid getting flagged or reported.

25. Avoid MySpace Violations - When using MySpace make sure you are not violating their terms of service with your specific use. Some sellers on MySpace appear to be violating the terms, although MySpace does not seem to police the activities with vigor..

10 Worst MySpace Practices

1. **Too Much Text!**   Like all good online and e-mail marketing and communications, the strategy is built upon less is more. Limit your "About Me" content in to four paragraphs that summarize your university and its academics, student/alumni life and athletics. Within these four paragraphs, hyperlink key words and drive your users to those sections on your website. The same is true for blogs, comments and bulletins. Your users want to scan your MySpace content, not read it.

2. **Too Much "Stuff" or Over-designed.** Once you are familiar with MySpace, you'll see that there is no

consistency in design and that there are very few user-unfriendly designs out there. In some cases the design is so poor that you can't even read their profile. Keep your design very simple and streamlined. Post no more than one or two slideshows and 4-5 videos. Keep it clean!

3. ***Boring Photos*** - Use photos that capture the efficacy of your products, the beauty of your campus, the uniqueness of your student life, and good athletics action shots. Also, be sure to provide a link to the virtual tour on your website!

4. ***Sending out Too Many Bulletins*** - One word… annoying. No more the one or two a day. Plan them in advance for a wide variety and to keep your bulletin marketing interesting.

5. ***Profiles that Lack HTML*** - You need to know HTML basics to properly design and use your MySpace. Hyperlinks are very important, know when to bold, and in some areas you'll need to know HTML images tags to insert your own photos. Additionally, you need to link to most important features on your website, such as the virtual tour, your alumni section, your course catalog, admissions, financial aid, etc.

6. ***Profiles that Don't Monitor Comments.*** There is a safety feature in MySpace that allows you to view comments before they are posted on your MySpace. Colleges and universities definitely need to this if you want to avoid improper language or photos posted on your MySpace. This is perhaps the number one reason why you should start a MySpace. If a current student or alum does it first, you have zero control over improper content on MySpace that markets your university.

7. ***Profiles that Don't Regularly Monitor their Top Friends.*** At least every couple of weeks you need to check the profiles of your top friends. They may have suddenly posted foul language or inappropriate photos. Although MySpace users understand that you didn't directly create this inappropriate content, they might think twice when they see you are featuring this content through your "Top Friends" function.

8. ***Profiles that Launch a Song or Video when Visited.*** MySpace has a feature that allows you to select a song that starts to play when your profile is visited. Don't use this feature. It's obviously fine for bands, musicians and music lovers, but not for colleges or universities. It's distracting, most often annoying, and will often prompt users to hit the "Back" button and exit your MySpace. Videos that load upon visiting your profile often crash browsers.

9. ***Trying Too Hard to be "Cool."*** Your MySpace profile is an extension of your website marketing. You have enough of the cool factor by having a MySpace profile and using YouTube. Don't try to be "cool" because MySpacers will see right through it and you will quickly progress to becoming "lame". The MySpace audience is diverse in age. Don't assume that you are just marketing to teenagers and that you need to teen talk. Your MySpace should be fun, but professional.

10. ***Profiles that Don't Integrate with the Overall Marketing Messages -*** Consistency is crucial. Use the key marketing messages and logos that are on your print materials and website. Most of your MySpace users will visit your website, and there should be a consistency.

"The only thing that interferes
with my learning
is my education."

– Albert Einstein

Chapter 5
Marketing with Digg

The fourth social media application we will discuss is Digg, a much different kind of social media site than Twitter, Facebook or MySpace. We will again ask and answer the following questions: What is Digg? What are its marketing applications? What are good tactics and best practices should be followed if using Digg ?

What is Digg?

Digg is a *social news website* which helps people discover and share content from anywhere on the Internet-- by submitting links and stories, and voting and commenting on the submitted links and stories. Voting stories up and down is the site's cornerstone function, respectively called *digging* and *burying.*

Many stories get submitted every day, but only the most *Dugg* stories appear on the front page. Digg's popularity has prompted the creation of other social networking sites with story submission and voting systems. From the biggest online destinations to the most obscure blog, Digg surfaces the best stuff as voted on by our users. You won't find editors at Digg because its there to provide a place where people can collectively determine the value of content and we're changing the way people consume information online.

A Quick Tour of Digg

How do they do this? Everything on Digg — from news to videos to images — is submitted by a community (that would be you). Once something is submitted, other people see it and Digg what they like best. If your submission rocks and receives enough Diggs, it is promoted to the front page for the millions of Digg visitors to see.

And it doesn't stop there. Because Digg is all about sharing and discovery, there's a conversation that happens around the content. Digg promotes that conversations and provides tools for its community to discuss the topics that they're passionate about. By looking at information through the lens of the collective community on Digg, you'll always find something interesting and unique. Digg is committed to giving every piece of content on the web an equal shot at being the next big thing.

Digg's original design was free of advertisements. As Digg became more popular, Google AdSense was added and now banners and display ads are available on the Digg website.

In May 2009, Digg launched a new feature called Facebook Connect. Facebook Connect allows users of Digg and Facebook to connect their accounts. When a Facebook account is connected to a Digg account, Digg articles can then be shared on the user's Facebook page. Facebook Connect also allows Facebook users to log into Digg with their Facebook account, bypassing the normally required Digg registration.

How Digg Works

"Digg is democratizing digital media." As a user, you participate in determining all site content by discovering, selecting, sharing, and discussing the news, and videos that appeal to you.

1. Discover

- *Submit your favorites.* Find an article, image, or video online and submit it to Digg.com. Your submission will immediately appear in "Upcoming Stories," where other members can find it and, if they like it, Digg it.

- *Become popular.* Once a submission has earned a critical mass of Diggs, it becomes "popular" and jumps to the homepage in its category. If it becomes one of the most popular, it qualifies as a "Top 10". If a submission doesn't receive enough Diggs within a certain time period, it eventually falls out of the "Upcoming" section.

- *Discover media on Digg.* Visit the "Upcoming" section to discover recently added news, and videos. Track submissions as they come in with Swarm, Stack, Big Spy or Arc, our real-time Flash visualization tools in Digg Labs. Or use Spy to watch the titles and descriptions as they roll down the page.

  Of course, you can always check the topic homepages to see what's newly popular. And you can subscribe to RSS   feeds of particular topics, popular/upcoming sections, individual users, and the search terms of your choice.

2. Select

- *Digg* - Participate in the collaborative editorial process by Digging the stuff that you like best. As you Digg, you contribute to the popularity of any given item. You also build a history of Digging that you or your friends can view.

- *Bury* - If you find stories with bad links, off-topic content, or duplicate entries, click "Bury." That's how we get the spam out of the system and let the good stuff rise to the top.

  The system only works when users actively participate on a large scale, so make sure to do your part and Digg and Bury content that matters to you!

3. Share

- *Build a network.* Invite your friends or find them on Digg and add them to your friends list. Your friends can then track what you're Digging and you can see what they Digg as well, enabling you to collectively find news together.

- *Email.* Send your friends (Diggers or non-Diggers) the stories that you Digg.

4. Discuss

- **_Comment._** Share your opinions by commenting on stories, images, and videos as well as Digging and Burying comments by other users.

Digg as a Marketing Tool

Digg can be a useful element of a digital marketing strategy for a number of reasons. For example, Digg can help you:

1. Spread Your Content

For those looking to spread your content and increase page views, Digg can be very effective, with most sites reporting _25,000 page views on a day that they reach the homepage._ This can be especially valuable if your site generates revenue from AdSense or a similar advertising program (although some people find that Digg users are less likely to click ads.)

Digg is a community based social network of people that spread the word for you. After all, how would 75 percent of the Diggers even know your article or post even existed if they weren't told about it by other Diggers? That's the power of social marketing. Whatever it is that you are marketing, whether it's a particular product or just a blog, you will find that you must get in touch with someone that will get in touch with 2 more people.

Digg can have a viral effect, and if used wisely and moderately it can be an effective marketing tool. Following are examples of the ways that you can use it to help market yourself and make friends that will read your blog.

▪ Important: look for articles of interest to you and others and be the first to Digg them. This can help get the attention of other Diggers.

▪ Comment on anything of interest. The funnier, wittier or more meaningful a comment is the more it will get Dugg and the more popular you will get.

▪ When you get Dugg, add the Digger of your story to your friends list. The more Diggers you get, the more friends you get.

▪ Instant Message the friends you have if they have similar interests. DON'T SPAM THEM. Simply make chit chat and find out what their interests are. Ask them about their blog or whatever they are interested in first. Most of the time they will ask you about yours which will give you an opportunity to let them check out your blog or website. Obviously, if your site is beneficial they will like it and subscribe to your feed.

▪ Once you post an article you have the opportunity to make a *shout* to your friends. This is the time to let them know about an article if you think it would be interesting to those on your friends list. Choose wisely and if you have been asked by a friend to not send shouts, then it would be best to abide to the request.

2. Generate Web Site Traffic

If your business depends heavily on visits to your web site, Digg may be an extremely important tool in your bag of marketing tactics.

That's because the most important marketing use of Digg probably relates to search engine optimization (SEO). Even if your content different than what Digg users would find interesting, Digg can still provide some very real benefits, but the more dug it is the better! Search engines, especially Google, seem to rely on social media sites to point toward quality content. Because users are allowed to vote on the best content this serves as an easy way to identify good content and filter out poor content. Can you use Digg to get an instant boost in your search engine rankings? Here are some steps to follow:

- **Select Key Words & Site Description**

    The most important part of the submission process is to put your keyword phrase that you selected earlier into the "Title" submission field. It doesn't have to be your exact phrase; for the example I gave above a title like "Find Advertising Rates online" would serve your purpose just as well. Be creative. For your description enter a short description of your site, but be sure to reiterate your keywords as well as a good sales pitch to get users to click (although it won't matter if they don't). Don't get carried away with your title and description, though, as Digg users are often apt to flag spam and advertisements as such.

- **Choose a Topic**

    Be especially careful in the next "choosing topic" section. As already mentioned, the goal here is to make your link stay on a front page of Digg for as long as possible. Be as specific as possible when selecting your category, but also pay attention to the amount of traffic each category receives. From the Digg homepage you can select different topics on the top navigation menu to view the front page for that topic and then view new stories by clicking the button at the top right labeled "upcoming". It is a good idea to research the activity of a few topics where you could paste your story. For example, you might have good results with your football sites by posting them to the football subsection. This category receives little normal activity and thus a link could stay on the upcoming football page for twelve hours or so. Once you have selected your category enter the code at the bottom and follow the rest of the pages to complete your story upload.

• **Google Page Ranking**

Why do you want to stay on a page as long as possible? That's where Google Page Rank comes in. Say that we went through the steps above for a football article. After submitting the link it will appear on the general upcoming article page as well as an upcoming football page. Your link won't stay on the general page for very long because so many articles are submitted to Digg, so Google probably won't see your link before it disappears. But your *link on the football page won't disappear as quickly* because there aren't as many football articles being submitted. Chances are if you stay there for at least half an hour Google will pick you up and give you credit for an authoritative link. This holds true for any category that you may submit to. If your content is really popular and gets enough Diggs it will move onto the "Popular" page for that category and then onto the front page of the entire website.

After Google picks up your high link from Digg the results

can be quite dramatic. When a user searches the keyword phrase that you placed in the title, your site will be included in the results. Your individual performance will vary with where you place in these results, but Digg links can temporarily propel some pages that were previously on the third page to the number one result. The effect generally loses steam after a few days and your ranking will begin to slip, but the temporary effect is very noticeable and will also contribute to a long term positioning.

Not only will your site rank higher for your selected keyword phrase, but Digg also provides another link in the Google search results where others can find your site. A link is created to the content's entry page on Digg and this link will often place high in search results as well because of Digg's authority. These links will linger around the second page for a less competitive search phrase, sometimes permanently ranking higher than your site's initial ranking ever was!

Tactics & Best Practices

1. Sign up for an Account - and plan to participate daily. A wishy-washy attitude will not work well with fellow Diggers.

2. Be sure you understand - how Digg works before you begin actively participating.

3. Pay attention to User Comments - be prepared to respond as well as become an active part of the conversation.

4. *Gauge What is Popular* - Get a feel for how and why certain stories become popular. This will give you a better understanding of Digg, and also give you insight into how to make your stories and postings more popular as well.

5. *Generate Friends* - Try to accumulate as many friends as you can. Much like Twitter, you want as many contacts and outreaches as you can garner so you can affect more people that way.

6. *Start a Buddy List* - This list is designed to give you a one-on-one ability within Digg. It allows IM use, but be careful and try to not use this feature too much or you'll turn people off.

7. *Build your profile* - make it look as thorough and professional as possible. Just like any other website or service, this is the home base where people will be looking to find out who you are and what you're about. Make it as good as you possibly can.

8. *Learn from Power Users* - Look for the power users of the site, and then be friends with them. This is a huge help to you because others will see that you're associated with them, and it will help you get much more exposure in the long run.

9. *Submit Good Content!* - Only submit content that is worth something. Don't bombard the site or your page with worthless links and silly stories. Make sure they are interesting and relevant.

10. Send out Shouts - On Digg, people can send out shouts to each other. This is the single best way to get noticed and to get some feedback, so send shouts often.

11. Ensure Good Keywords - Keywords are very important. Just like any articles or information on your website, keywords are what get peoples' attention, so think some through and then use them in your posting title and in your content.

12. Aim to Become a Top User. The top users on this website get the most notice.

13. Do your Homework - Find out what people are talking about and then expand on that with your own postings.

14. Learn the Language - and how people express themselves. Every website has its own unique lingo that users pick up on, so be sure you are in the know.

15. Be Selective - Only keep friends who provide feedback, who link to you, and whom you can link to as well. Get rid of any friends who are just idle or who are not contributing.

16. Continuously Improve Content - Try to dedicate yourself to taking time each and every day to focus on content expansion and editing. Dedicating this time will really reflect on your profile.

17. Keep Up - on what the Digg users like and hate. For example, most users love Apple products, but hate Microsoft (as a whole). Get a feeling for the pulse of what is popular.

18. *Learn the Demographics* - Overall, there are more male than female users on Digg. Get an idea of the demographics of the site so you can have more success.

19. *Be Relevant Always* - Relevant content is important, and currently topics like the environment, science, breaking news, politics, technology, and comedy are hot topics. Use these in relation to your business somehow, so that people will want to know more.

20. *Vote Judiciously* - Do not vote thumbs up on too many of your own articles. This can raise a red flag and could potentially get your account removed.

21. *Be Impressive* - Make your title WOW viewers and visitors. This is your first line to people and the best way to get noticed and get some Diggs.

22. *Write Great Descriptions* - Descriptions are also important, so be sure to write these well and with important keywords included.

23. *Use Real Numbers* - *instead of written numbers. This really does get more atte*ntion than a lot of people realize.

24. *Digg It!* Try not to just comment on stories. Remember the purpose of Digg, and if you like something, Digg away!

25. *Avoid Spamming* - people with keywords. They are very important, but too many of one particular thing can drive people away almost instantly. Savvy users know spam when they see it, so DON'T DO IT!

78

26. English Only, Please - Do not use any non-English websites or content. The temptation to post some Chinese language website links to reach out to global users might be really strong, but it's not allowed on the website since it is an English speaking only site.

27. Subscribe to the RSS Feed offered by Digg - so you can keep up with the latest updates and see what the most popular post is.

28. Plan Forward - Check the upcoming stories, link to other's postings, and push your way up to the top by recommending others and making as many friends as you can.

29. Write about Digg. Although this may sound a little redundant, fans of Digg actually want to hear more about how to get the most out of the website.

30. Discuss the Latest Technology - since many people who use the site are big fans of the latest applications, websites, and electronics. Firefox noticed a large influx of users after people discussed them on Digg, and this can happen for your business as well.

31. Digg Town Halls - Participate in the Digg Town Halls. The site now has occasional town hall style discussions, where you can share information, ask questions, and meet new users.

32. Relevant, Original Content - Be sure your content is a must see. Try to post things that have not been put up before, and make them intriguing and tantalizing. Again, this is where the effective title writing comes into play.

33. Diggs Content - Unlike some other sites, users on Digg do not like for you to ask for Diggs. Instead, let your content speak for itself.

34. Be Selective with Friends - Try to be selective about your friends. Too many friends will be overwhelming, and your inbox will get overloaded. It's good to have a lot of contacts and friends, but too many can actually be a bad thing because it takes up way too much of your space and time. Choose friends who will do you a favor, just as you will do for them.

35. Be Selective on Diggs! Do not Digg every single thing you see. By Digging every little posting, you look less legitimate, and you're giving certain people more credit than they actually deserve. The goal is to Digg content that is relevant and well put together, not just everyone's postings.

36. Get Diggs - Remind people to Digg your stuff from other sites, like your blogs. Be Selective on your home page.

37. Don't Overdo Posts - Submit a good amount of posts, but don't overdo it. Some people will submit so much content every day that they overload the website and their profile. It's not an attractive habit, and it can make people leery. Instead, only post a few, select things per day.

38. Analyze! Think about the numbers involved with Digg, such as the number of hits per hour, number of buries, and the number of popular articles that have hit within the last day or so. All of these statistics and more are important and help you gain a better grasp of your progress.

39. Get Help if Needed - Don't try to do it all on your own. If you're a very busy business owner or website host, recruit coworkers and friends to help post some things on**48. Easy on *Caveat Emptor*** - Do not make baseless claims. If you post some topics or information, do not make promises you cannot keep. It's never a good idea to sound like a salesman or make pitches for things people may not want. Instead, entice them to your site to make a purchase with relevant content.

40. Buzz. Buzz, Buzz - Utilize the newest buzz on Digg to your advantage. While you never want to copy others' content, you can use the popular topics to give you fresh ideas that will rope people in.

41. Have Fun!! While the purpose of using Digg in this context is to expand your business and gain new contacts, remember to have fun!

42. Digg. As long as they follow your own personal guidelines for posting, it can be a huge help.

43. Pictures are a Thousand Words - Be sure to include a picture for a thumbnail. Choose something that will get peoples' attention and make a statement, as well as something that defines who you are.

44. Widgets - Widgets are an awesome new way to get more people reading. These can be personalized so you can make them all your own, and they really add personality to your page.

45. *Merchandise Digg* - Add the Digg button, image and all, to your company or personal website.

46. Make Content Easy to Digest - Numbered lists make for easy reading, and keep peoples' interest. Write some content with top 10 lists, or other forms of numbered lists, which create small tidbits of information.

47. *Once Again, Learn From the Big Boys* - Keep in mind that the top 100 users on Digg control over half of the website's content ranking. Pay close attention to what they are looking at and commenting on.

48. *Stand Out from the Crowd* - Be as unique and individual as you can. Try to stay with the feel of the site, but go against the flow with your content.

49. *Be Open.* The users of Digg are pretty open, honest, and out there when it comes to how they feel about things. If you do not like something, don't feel like you cannot express it. Just do so with a bit of discretion so you are not bashing people or businesses to the point of no return.

50. *Tailor Topics to Audience* - Focus on your audience, and decide what topics are of the most interest to them.
###

Chapter 6
Marketing on LinkedIn

The fifth social media opportunity we shall examine is LinkedIn, a site dedicated to businesses and professionals. As before, we will ask, "What is LinkedIn? What are its most important marketing applications? What are the best tactics and best practices for using it?

What is LinkedIn?

LinkedIn is a business-oriented social networking site founded in December 2002 and launched in May 2003-- mainly to be used for professional networking. As of July 2009, it had more than 43 million registered users, spanning 170 industries.

LinkedIn's CEO is Jeff Weiner, previously a Yahoo! Inc. executive. On June 17, 2008, Sequoia Capital, Greylock Partners, and oth venture capital firms purchased a 5% stake in the company for $53 million, giving the company a post-money valuation of approximately $1 billion.

FREE MARKETING WITH SOCIAL MEDIA

The purpose of the LinkedIn site is to allow registered users to maintain a list of contact details of people they know and trust in business. The people in the list are called Connections. Users can invite anyone (whether a site user or not) to become a connection.

This list of connections can then be used in a number of ways.

- A contact network is built up consisting of their direct connections, the connections of each of their connections (termed second-degree connections) and also the connections of second-degree connections (termed third-degree connections). This can be used to gain an introduction to someone you wish to know through a mutual, trusted contact.

- It can then be used to find jobs, people and business opportunities recommended by someone in one's contact network.

- Employers can list jobs and search for potential candidates.

- Job seekers can review the profile of hiring managers and discover which of their existing contacts can introduce them.

The "gated-access approach" (where contact with any professional requires either a preexisting relationship or the intervention of a contact of theirs) is intended to build trust among the service's users. LinkedIn participates in EU's International Safe Harbor Privacy Principles.

The feature LinkedIn Answers, similar to Google Answers or Yahoo! Answers, allows users to ask questions for the community to answer. This feature is free and the main differences from the latter two services are that questions are potentially more business-oriented, and the identity of the people asking and answering questions is known.

The searchable LinkedIn Groups, feature allows users to establish new business relationships by joining alumni, industry, or professional and other relevant groups. LinkedIn groups can be created in any subjects and by any member of LinkedIn. Some groups are specialized groups dealing with a narrow domain or industry whereas others are very broad and generic in nature.

The newest LinkedIn feature is LinkedIn Polls, still in alpha.

In addition, a mobile version of the site was launched in February 2008 which gives access to a reduced feature set over a mobile phone. The mobile service is available in six languages: Chinese, English, French, German, Japanese and Spanish.

In mid-2008, LinkedIn launched LinkedIn DirectAds as a form of sponsored advertising.

In October, 2008, LinkedIn enabled an "applications platform" that allows other online services to be embedded within a member's profile page. For example, among the initial applications were an Amazon Reading List that allows LinkedIn members to display books they are reading and a Six Apart, WordPress and TypePad application that allows members to display their latest blog postings within their LinkedIn profile.

LinkedIn as a Marketing Tool

With the dizzying number of social networking sites that have sprung up in recent years, trying to select the most worthwhile for your business can be a daunting task.

However, there is one that stands out if you are an entrepreneur, a business owner, or a professional. LinkedIn is the ONE social network that you. The goal for any business person joining LinkedIn is not to add friends and swap stories and pictures, but rather, to make new business connections.

Following are some of the ways your business could benefit from joining LinkedIn and developing a relationship with other businesses.

1. Generate More Business

As soon as you start networking, you increase your chances of reaching new customers. However, be prepared and be willing to work at it. If you're not into social media and don't want to put in the time and effort to network in several sites at the same time, this is the ONE site you should focus on. You may not see it at first, but with the combined use of several strategies and tips, you should benefit from more business.

2. Study the Competition

With the use of LinkedIn you can see your competitors' teams, clients, and references, plenty of information that is not readily available to you otherwise. You may also see where they're coming from, or what they've been up to recently.

3. Obtain Greater Visibility

Linkedin provides options that will allow your profile to be indexed by search engines, like Google. Make use of these options and your business will achieve greater visibility on the

Web.

4. Conduct Market Research

If you're considering launching a new product, you can see what type of demand there is for this type of product. Do research on what companies are offering. Make use of the Q&A feature to post your questions.

5. Facilitate Professional Introductions

With LinkedIn, you can ask the people you already know to introduce you to someone you'd like to know. This gives you greater credibility and improves your chances of actually getting that meeting you want.

6. Show Recommendations

You may not only view what recommendations others have received, but essentially encourage those you've done business with to recommend your services or products. Then people who read your profile have the opportunity to see why others recommend you.

So, if Facebook and MySpace are not your cup of tea, LinkedIn is the business to business social networking site you'll feel most comfortable with if you wish to promote your business and services and build business relationships that will prove profitable to everyone involved. All 500 of the Fortune 500 are represented in LinkedIn. And the above-mentioned benefits are the reasons why.

Tactics & Best Practices

1. ***Clarify Your Area of Expertise*** - Check the expertise requests option in your profile.

2. ***Detail Profile*** - Complete your profile as thoroughly as possible, and include interests, an avatar, and business information.

3. ***Network with Business Associates*** - Connect with as many business associates as you can, since they will help you to network with like minded individuals and companies.

4. ***Learn from Others*** - Gain new knowledge, so you can become an expert in other subjects and topics.

5. ***Ask Questions!!!*** You may be deluged with answers and advice from other professionals providing their own perspectives.

6. ***Answer Questions.*** Use your knowledge to your advantage by answering peoples' questions thoroughly and expertly, and you'll gain other users' confidence.

7. ***Check in Often*** - Check your home page on LinkedIn fairly often. It contains industry updates, news, and postings from associates.

8. ***Be Observant*** - On company profiles, the top five most popular other profiles are displayed on the home page. This is important since it will show others who you associate with, so be aware of who your top five are.

9. ***Reciprocity*** - Choose the top 5 who will link back to you,

so there is a reciprocal benefit.

10. ***Detail Work Experience*** - Be sure to explain your work experience in as much detail as possible. Don't just list employers or experience, but instead expand upon it by showing others' what you've done in detail.

11. ***Discussion Forums*** - Comment in the discussion forums as much as you can so your profile gets noticed.

12. ***Update your Status*** - with useful content and information as much as possible.

13. ***Integrate Keywords for Searches*** - Feel free to implement keywords in both your profile and your content, so that your information comes up in search engine results.

14. ***Include Link Elsewhere*** - Do not forget to include your LinkedIn profile link in other places like Twitter, Digg, and other social media websites.

15. ***Use as Recruitment Tool*** - LinkedIn is also a useful employment tool, so if you're hiring, use it to find good employees.

16. ***Customize your Buttons.*** This will make your profile look more professional and give you more control.

17. ***Emphasize Skills*** - Include your skills and specialties and be sure to expand upon your current business.

18. ***Include Key Information in Profile*** - Obviously, include your company URL somewhere on your profile.

19. ***Have a Plan*** - in place when you begin to build your

network, otherwise you may end up getting some contacts you don't want, and not enough of the ones you do.

20. ***Be Selective*** - Do not just be friends with people because they ask you to. It looks a little odd for a professional member to be friend with their partying buddies from college. Leave the casual online friendships to Facebook.

21. ***Analysis*** - Look at network statistics to see what is going on with your account and the progress you're making.

22. ***Use Characters in Profile Wisely*** - Keep in mind the number of characters in profile fields are limited, so you may want to do a few practice runs first before publishing everything.

23. ***Include History in Profile*** - Include past education and past companies/experience, not just your current business or company.

24. ***Customize URLs*** - Customize your public profile's URL so it's easier to link this to other pages and people will remember it much better.

25. ***Due Diligence*** - Utilize the reference check tool to find out how long someone worked for a company and much more.

26. **Seek Advice** - Ask others within the community for advice. Since this site was designed for networking, people are usually more than willing to answer questions and give help.

27. ***Study the Competition*** - Use the site to help get a much clearer picture of your competition.

28. ***Cultivate Others*-** Compliment others and give them praise when you're speaking to them, so that they reciprocate. It makes both of your profiles look much better and can increase your exposure and ratings.

29. ***Be Results Oriented*** - Do not only mention what you've done, but include what you've produced. Be sure to post results from your actions and include facts and figures if possible.

30. ***Use Numbers*** - Show people and percentages as actual, real numbers that back up the claims of your success.

31. ***Have a Dynamite Summary*** - The top of your summary is what visitors see first so be certain you're including the most vital information here.

32. ***Answers Tool*** - Utilize the answers tool as an opportunity to show off you expertise.

33. ***LinkedIn Resources*** - If you're in need of a graphic designer, web hosting provider, or any other service, LinkedIn has its own services area where you can trade off with others who are in the trusted network.

34. ***Blog Links*** - Use your LinkedIn page link in your blogs, Twitter, Digg, your website, etc.

35. ***Performance*** - Try to become a recommended service or company by establishing a good reputation. People will flock more towards ones that have the "recommended" status.

36. *Profile Enabling* - Be sure to enable the "show website" feature in your profile.

37. *Web Site View* - Make sure the full view and websites options are also checked so that the information in your profile is public.

38. *Targeting* - LinkedIn is mostly designed for targeted marketing, so be as specific as you can when you choose your industry and expertise.

39. **Make Connections** - Use the website as a tool to make connections within your business niche, and then expand upon those connections on other social media sites.

40. *Build Network* - Be willing to work at building your network; it takes time to get a lot of solid connections.

41. *Search Engines* - Make use of the option to be indexed so your information appears on Google and other search engines' results.

42. *Ask for Opinions* - Use the Q&A feature to ask others their opinion of your website, product, etc.

43. *Introduce Yourself* - Feel free to introduce yourself to other members. Don't always wait for others to approach you first.

44. *Recommendations* - Ask others to recommend you if they have had experience with you.

45. *Home Base* - Think of LinkedIn as your "home base" for all of your other marketing tactics.

46. *Stay Up to Date* - Edit your profile often and rearrange things as needed, so you are always up to date and new content is there as well.

47. *Use the Groups Feature* - to meet others, post feedback, and get a feel for what other companies are up to.

48. *To Begin Building Network* - Start your network base with people you know and trust, and build from there.

49. *Always be Professional with Professionals* - Be as professional as possible at all times.

50. *Spelling & Grammar* – It should go without saying that part of being professional is to always be aware of spelling and grammar.

"If content is King,
then conversion
is Queen."

--John Munsell, CEO Bizzuka

Chapter 7
Marketing with Squidoo

The sixth social media opportunity is Squidoo. So, what in the world is a Squidoo? What are Squidoo's major marketing applications? What are some important best practices to follow when using Squidoo?

What is Squidoo?

Squidoo is a community website that allows users to create pages (called lenses) for subjects of interest. Squidoo is in the top 500 most visited sites in the world, and is in the top 300 most viewed in the United States. Squidoo grew 91% in 2008, and had 900,000 hand built lenses as of February 1st, 2009. Over 400,000 people reportedly visit Squidoo every day.

Development on Squidoo started in 2005, launching a beta testing period in October of that year. The site came out of beta testing two months later and reached 100,000 lenses within the first six months. As stated previously, Squidoo now has more than 900,000 lenses and grew 91% in 2008.

Squidoo is a user-generated website which uses the concept of a lens as its primary feature. Lenses are much like a blog posts, except on a single subject. The site allows content creators to earn revenue from referral links to sites like Amazon.com and Ebay. The users who create lenses, called "lensmasters," can be anyone with an interest in a specific subject; they do not necessarily have to be externally-recognized experts.

Squidoo is notable in that it allows users to create multimedia pages without learning HTML. These pages often achieve built-in popularity due to their association with thousands of other Squidoo pages.

The site also employs a unique payment scheme. For example, 5% of its revenue goes to charity, 50% goes to the lensmasters, and 45% goes to Squidoo. The lens and Squidoo rely on advertising and affiliate links to create revenue. Nearly half of lensmasters donate their royalties to any of 65 featured charities, ranging from NPR and the American Heart Association to smaller organizations like Chimp Haven and Planet Gumbo. In October 2008, Squidoo donated $80,000 to charity.

So, Squidoo is a popular on line platform for producing lenses -- small websites, or one page sites-- that focus on a particular business, book, or hobby. (Thanks to Wikipedia for the background).

Squidoo as a Marketing Tool

Is a customer looking for you on line and cannot find you? Maybe you need a Squidoo lens!

A Squidoo Lens is a popular marketing tool that allows people to create small websites (lenses) to communicate via free web pages. A single web page is called a Squidoo lens.
No technical knowledge is required to create a Squidoo lens. With no prior web building skills anyone can build a lens in about 10 minutes. All one needs to do is to click the "Create a Lens" button and follow along with the wizard.

Besides being free and easy to set up, setting up a Squidoo lens or two has many benefits for internet marketers.

1. ***Affiliate Links.*** For starters, Squidoo is one of the few websites that allows affiliate links. This accepting attitude towards online businesses makes it easier to establish yourself as a Squidoo community member as opposed to other websites that sub their nose at online marketers. You can join the site knowing you are allowed to use Squidoo to promote your own podcasts, blog or websites.

2. ***Search Engine Traffic.*** Search engines, especially Google, love Squidoo. Because Google is such a key player in the amount and type of traffic your site receives, it should please you to know that Squidoo search results tend to come up in Google ahead of all the social bookmarking sites. Using Squidoo can increase your search engine ranking and the traffic you receive to your site. The more lenses you make, the more your website ranking will improve.

3. ***Polling.*** Squidoo lets you set up polls on your lens. Anyone can do it and they are not complicated to set up. Doing so lets you gain some valuable insight into your niche markets. You can ask readers about products they use, get reviews about products they bought and so much more. The answers you can get by using the poll module can help you to build a better business. You can even ask questions and then link to other lens providing the answers. It's an interactive way to get some great niche insight.

4. ***Host Auctions, Sales.*** A Squidoo lens can also host eBay auctions, Amazon books, YouTube Videos etc. These are assets that many marketers use to build their web business. If someone clicks on your Amazon link, for instance, you earn a royalty.

5. ***Test Key Words & Phrases.*** A Squidoo lens is a good way to test out keyword phrases for popularity and web traffic. Your Squidoo dashboard provides statistics, including the number of visits your lens has received in the last seven days. You can see which of your lists is most popular. This information is very valuable when you're optimizing your lens.

6. ***Be a Content Provider.*** Besides earning money by promoting your affiliate program or eBay shop you can also earn by being a Squidoo content provider or lensmaster as they are referred to in the Squidoo community. Basically the way it works is when you create a page and Squidoo runs ads on them you get a cut of the revenue generated when a reader clicks on an ad.

You can also earn by promoting Squidoo through their affiliate program. Once you get an account you get a referral link. Once someone who signs up under you earns their first $15 you receive $5. A Squidoo lens is a highly recommended marketing technique for internet marketers. Above are some of the benefits that it poses especially for those who work from home.

Do You Squidoo?

Do you Squidoo? It may sound racy, but Squidoo is actually a helpful marketing tool for Web site owners interested in driving traffic through social media. While Squidoo doesn't allow for too much interaction between users like Twitter or Facebook, it can integrate other social networks and popular sites to create a dynamic online place card for any topic imaginable.

The unusual Squidoo logo, that of a squid-like creature bearing one all-seeing eye, best personifies the site in that its many tentacles represents the infinite number of modules one can place in a Squidoo page. Pages, better known as "lenses" among enthusiasts, are comprised of different widgets that permit the user to add different functionalities and content sections on the topic of choice. While it may sound daunting, creating a Squidoo lens to complement your main Web site is probably one of the easiest ways to help boost your inbound link popularity.

Creating a Squidoo Lens

Once you have registered as a member (it costs nothing), you are cleared to create your first lens. The simple creation wizard walks you through entering information that the lens will convey, and the vanity URL suffix that will display on launch. Let's say you own a baseball memorabilia store and wish to create a lens on rare baseball cards. That will be your main topic, and a URL you could use might be "rare-baseball-cards" if it is available.

Novice users have the option of allowing Squidoo to choose starter modules in which you add content. These may be widgets connected to online bookstores and auction sites, photo galleries like Flickr, or simple text modules for articles. Advanced users can take advantage of a freer option that lets you create the lens from scratch. Suggested modules for your first lens include.

1. *Text Modules.* Here you write about your products/topic, and include keyword-rich links back to your main site.

2. *Link Modules.* If you have an interest in a number of related sites, you can group them in this module as a handy reference.

3. *Video Modules.* Enhance your lens with embedded YouTube clips.

4. *RSS Modules.* Have a blog? Feed the RSS into your Squidoo lens and you will update this lens as you make new posts.

5. *Twitter Modules.* Similar to the RSS, you can add your Twitter information to post on Squidoo and in turn attract new followers.

Once you have all the modules in place (you'll need at least four or five before Squidoo will allow you to go live), you can publish your lens for public consumption. With just the click of a button, you can add your lens information to a variety of social networks and stimulate interest in your content. The beauty of Squidoo, too, is that you are not limited to the number of pages you can make -

create a lens for every aspect of your business, condense articles into modules and add related photo and video widgets, and you can turn simple Web content into a dynamic social tool that can increase awareness of your brand.

Tactics & Best Practices

1. ***Create a Great Lens*** - Make sure your page on Squidoo is its absolute best! A polished page gets more results.

2. ***Promote, Promote, Promote!*** Don't be afraid to promote and market your business and website through your profile or content.

3. ***Title your Lenses Effectively -*** A great title and the right keyw keywords will get attention.

4. ***Have an Effective Introduction*** - Make the introduction and description captivating and helpful so people want to read more.

5. ***Add Photos*** - for visual interest in the description.

6. ***Set up multiple lenses*** - for multiple keyword phrases. This is highly recommended.

7. ***Use Tags to your Advantage-*** Do so by making the most effective tags possible using powerful wording and linking to the best sites that will get you real results.

8. ***Understand the Link Flow on Squidoo*** - so you know how people find you, and how your links get distributed from the source page.

9. *Make a "Lens of the Day"* - to keep people interested in your page and they'll want to see what you have to say more often.

10. *Find your Voice on Squidoo* - Think about who you are and what you're trying to accomplish. Brainstorm some content ideas and think about your plans in advance before setting up your profile and lenses.

11. *Credibility* - Be sure you are not only knowledgeable about your content, but that it comes across that way to others.

12. *Ensure Good Grammar* - As always, watch spelling, grammar, and use of language.

13. *Patience* - The key with this website as with any other, so do things right the first time, and don't expect results overnight.

14. *Learn from Others* - Use the forum to your advantage to get advice, see what others are doing, and ask and answer questions

15. *No Spam* - Do not spam your pages or lenses, as people will run away from your profile. Members can tell spam a mile away.

16. *First Lens* - Make a lens solely about you, so people have a place to start.

17. *Co-branding* - is popular and a great way to get more income. Find some other companies or brands you can partner up with.

18. ***Use the Squidoo Answer Deck*** - if you have any questions or need help.

19. ***Use Squidcast to Promote*** - The Squidcast feature lets you promote your lenses, so definitely use this to your advantage.

20. ***Check your Links*** - Make sure all of your links work. You should check them periodically to ensure they still work.

21. ***Update Links*** - If time goes on and you find better links, don't forget to update them!

22. ***Add a Table of Contents to your Lens*** - People really like this feature!

23. ***Spell Check***, spell check, spell check.

24. ***Update your Profile*** - to allow people to contact you so that you are available to your customers, potential clients, and anyone who want to ask you something. Being accessible is a great way to gain a good reputation.

25. ***Cross Promote on Twitter*** - Twitter is a great tool for promoting your lenses, so use it to your advantage.

26. ***Edit your Modules*** - so they are not just the ones generated from Squidoo. Tailor them to each lens, so it looks more through and professional.

27. ***The More Lenses the Better*** - The more high quality lenses you have, the better so make up as many as you can. Just be sure each one has a purpose and will get results.

28. ***Your Mission Statement = Lens Title*** - Think of ways to spin your company's mission statement into a lens title.

29. ***Tie in with Charities*** - Charities play a big role on Squidoo. Find a few you believe in, and work with them on your pages.

30. ***Point Lenses to Many Places*** - Don't just limit lenses to links. Have them point to your RSS feeds, Twitter, Flickr page, and tons more.

31. ***Cross Promote*** - If you're a fan of other companies or products, make a lens for it. See if the place you're a fan of will reciprocate the favor.

32. ***Use Referrals to your Advantage -*** Recruit as many people as you can.

33. ***Communicate your Affiliate Program*** - Don't hesitate to make a lens about your own affiliate program.

34. ***Get Affiliates to Help*** - Have your affiliates make some lenses of their own promoting your website.

35. ***Watch Spam Guidelines!*** - Don't forget that spam is NOT welcome on Squidoo, and your account could be canceled if you spam. Find out about their guidelines before publishing anything.

36. ***Use Google AdSense*** – Use Adsense in conjunction with Squidoo, since they work hand in hand.

37. ***Max your Lenses for Optimum Exposure.*** Simply check

this option on the edit pages of your lenses for the maximum view and exposure.

38. ***Aspire to Earn the Giant Badge*** - so people will see you've been a longstanding member who produces quality content.

39. ***Earn Gold Stars*** - Try to get gold stars for your lenses, as this means you're the best of the best.

40. ***Use the Flickr Module to Incorporate Cool Photos*** - Visually appealing lenses and modules typically have the most success.

41. ***Add your Squidoo Links*** - to your blogs and website.

42. ***Add Squidoo Groups*** - Add your lenses to Squidoo groups. Look into the many different groups available and then add your lenses accordingly.

43. ***Use the Forums*** - Introduce yourself in the Forums, and on other websites dedicated to Squidoo users.

44. ***Patience*** - The longer you're on Squidoo, the better your reputation, so remember it takes a while to become established.

45. ***Have Unique Lenses*** - The more lenses the better; just make sure each is unique in its own way.

46. ***Paypal*** - Make sure you have a Paypal account, because that is how Squidoo makes payments.

47. ***Content, Content, Content*** - Your content should be thorough and high quality. Don't skimp on well written

105

content just to get more lenses published.

48. ***Use Research from Multiple Sources*** - Do not just use Google as a resource for information when creating content. Look into more in depth resources and you content will be much better.

49. ***Updating Lenses*** - It's up to you how often you want to update your lenses. As long as they remain relevant, it's OK to leave them alone.

50. ***Use Popular Hot Topics for Lenses*** - Aside from your own company or business related topics. It still gets hits!

###

Chapter 8
Marketing with StumbleUpon

The seventh social media opportunity we will discuss-- StumbleUpon-- is truly a unique social media concept. As before, we will ask, "What is StumbleUpon? What are its primary marketing applications? What are the best tactics and best practices to follow when using StumbleUpon?"

What is StumbleUpon?

StumbleUpon is an internet community that allows its users to discover and rate web pages, photos, and videos. It has a personalized recommendation engine which uses peer and social networking principles to rate submissions.

StumbleUpon was owned by eBay from May 2007 (when it was

acquired for $75,000,000) until April 2009, when two of the founders, backed by investors, bought it back.

Web pages are presented when the user clicks the "Stumble!" button on the browser's toolbar. StumbleUpon chooses which Web page to display based on the user's ratings of previous pages, ratings by his/her friends, and by the ratings of users with similar interests. Users can rate or choose not to rate any Web page with a thumbs up or thumbs down, and clicking the Stumble button resembles "channel-surfing" the Web. StumbleUpon also allows their users to indicate their interests from a list of nearly 500 topics to produce relevant content for the user. There is also one-click blogging built in as well.

StumbleUpon as a Marketing Tool

Users/Audience

StumbleUpon has approximately 5 million users, i.e., people who have registered and 5 billion Stumbles. That number is kind of meaningless, though, because it counts anyone who has ever registered for the Website.

Marketing Applications of StumbleUpon

StumbleUpon can primarily be used as a tool to increase traffic to a web site. Here are the basic steps to follow.

1. **Sign Up**
   Sign up for a free account at Stumbleupon.com. Click on the "Add StumbleUpon to My Browser" link and provide your email address and a user name and password. Enter

your birthday, gender, and type the words in that appear in the text box. Click on the "Join and Download Now" button.

2. Install Toolbar

Install the StumbleUpon toolbar to your browser. At StumbleUpon.com, click on the "Download now – Free" button on the right under the "Get the StumbleUpon Toolbar" title.

3. Login

Login to Stumbleupon.com with your user name and password from Step 1. Confirm that the Stumbleupon toolbar is installed on the top of the Internet browser window.

4. Stumble

StumbleUpon your website by clicking on the thumbs up. Stumbling is like discovering and bookmarking a favorite website. By adding a link to your website, you are creating a backlink to your site, which helps with search engine optimization and traffic. When the large StumbleUpon community clicks on the "Stumble" button in their toolbars, they may come across your website. This can improve your traffic significantly.

5. Make friends

Make friends by stumbling other websites that you like. Click on the "Stumble" button on the toolbar to find websites, then click on the thumbs up "I like it" button to stumble the site. Some website owners will return the favor by visiting, stumbling, and recommending your site. It's also a great way to discover great websites, blogs, and videos.

StumbleUpon does not replace search or sites like Digg – they are their own beast due to their collaborative filtering/recommendation engine. StumbleUpon is like Amazon's recommendations, but for web pages and video.

As indicated previously, StumbleUpon hit 5 million users. Some observations:

1. Competitively they're not trying to beat search... they're "taking on television," according to one observor.

2. StumbleUpon will eventually have a bidding model, but right now have a 5 cents a click flat rate. That is, they are cheap right now.

3. An API is in the works. When StumbleUpon starts to splinter through APIs you want to know already how to market here.

Now, for some suggested principles for how to market unpaid in StumbleUpon.

1. You must inform and entertain with laser targeting and a high WOW factor. Piper Jaffray calls it *communitainment*. SEOs call it link bait; others call it branded content that converts visitors to subscribers/linkers/buyers.

2. Don't just submit content – join the community (much as you would for Digg) and spend time learning what your target community likes. StumbleUpon recently added profiles and community networks much like MySpace

and MyBlogLog. There are records of what community members like. If your content lacks the WOW power of what they like then you've got to get back to work.

3. Pictures are important.

And here are three thoughts if you're interested in how to market with sponsored Stumbles:

1. All the unpaid rules apply.

2. If you're investing serious effort into your content – ie, you've paid someone $5k+ to write link bait for you – why not spend $200 dollars more and send it through SU?

3. What you're really paying for in this instance is access to the results, and though this won't tell you WHAT to change, you should get an idea of whether or not your new project WOWs your target community.

4. Camp suggested you pay for stumbles on content that's quality but that people aren't necessarily searching for... Audio/Visual content works well he said, as do cool flash pages.

5. If you're launching a site and have invested in branded content that's intended to convert viewers into linkers, subscribers or buyers then SU should ABSOLUTELY be on your list of places to advertise. If your market is there of course... Check out the SU Buzz page, which shows you recent stumbles (in a very Digg-looking format) along with a list along the left side of your screen of SU categories.

Following are some observations and tips on marketing via

StumbleUpon.

1. ***StumbleUpon Sponsored Stumbles vs. Google AdWords-*** StumbleUpon can be a great alternative to click based traffic in the sense that you get a continuous stream of interested visitors. The traffic is also qualified in the sense that the visitors said they were interested in your topic or category.

2. ***How to Use StumbleUpon for Your Business-*** "Why should you look at into directing StumbleUpon traffic to your site? Beyond the obvious benefits of extremely targeted traffic, the traffic doesn't come all at once compared to a site like Digg."

3. ***How to Get StumbledUpon -*** "If you want to get a lot of traffic to your site from StumbleUpon, make sure you have a lot of friends before you start voting."

More Tactics & Best Practices

1. ***Your Web Site -*** Make sure your website is up to par. Since people will be "stumbling upon" your site, you want to make sure it looks really good as soon as they click on the link.

2. ***Build Network -*** Just like Twitter, StumbleUpon is a social networking website, so be sure to get as many contacts and networking friends as possible.

3. ***Your Profile -*** Complete your profile as thoroughly as possible before linking. This way, when people click on

your information, they get an idea of who you are or who your business is.

4. ***Cover as Many Bases as Possible in the Profile.*** Try not to leave too many stones unturned, so people know exactly what you're about from the get go.

5. ***Links!!*** - Leave links on as many sites as possible. You want people to link right back to you, so link up!

6. ***Be Careful Where you Stumble***. Remember that people can see the path of links that you've followed, and they will have gotten to you by following a particular path. Don't link to places or people you do not want to be associated with or you will turn visitors off.

7. ***Utilize Those Keywords!*** Use an SEO service or writer to help you place the best and most effective keywords possible. This is truly the key to getting your information stumbled upon.

8. ***Tag the Most Essential Elements.*** StumbleUpon uses tags, which are a lot like keywords. Be sure to tag your site using the most effective, power packing tags possible. Try to pick nouns and use ones that will pique peoples' interest immediately. While you must use one topic on the site, you can use multiple tags and change them up as needed.

9. ***Use Your Friends for Help.*** The website has a feature that lets you contact your friends and inform them of your topic. They will see a notification on their toolbar. While this is fun and a good way to gather up more people, do not abuse it or else you may end up annoying people rather than informing them.

10. ***Quality Over Quantity*** - Do not focus so much on becoming a huge "stumbler", but rather focus on the quality of your topics and posts. If you worry too much about your followers or your rating, you may end up neglecting the content, which is really what's important.

11. ***Make a commitment*** - Decide right away that you're going to be an important part of the StumbleUpon web community, and then stick with it. Feeble posters or people who are fly by night are easy to detect, and most people will stay away from that.

12. ***Review and Rate as Many Others' Sites as Possible*** - So that you are perceived as an active member and not just standing on the sidelines.

13. ***Long Posts/Many Links*** - Try to create long posts with as many links as possible. This garners you more content, more referrals, and more chances to get noticed.

14. ***Don't Overdo the Ads!*** - Try not to "kill" your page with ads or spam. This is usually an automatic turn off for people who might stumble upon your page. Keep those pesky ads at bay if at all possible!

15. ***Target Your Audience*** - Think about your target audience. Then, create customized content just for them. By putting information out there that caters to your audience and your customer base, you will get solid followers who should turn into sales or referrals.

16. ***A Great Title is Worthy 1000 Words!*** - Make sure you write a captivating and effective title, and a good introductory

paragraph. Most people look at the title first and foremost, so make sure it is one that will grab their attention and make them want to read more.

17. ***Thank the People who Stumble to You.*** This has a very positive effect and usually gets people to recommend your page to others.

18. ***Join Communities -*** That are in relation to your business. You just might learn something, and by getting involved in communities with like-minded people, you might discover some really useful contacts.

19. ***Keep it Fresh.*** Try to post new articles daily, if not weekly. You want the content to stay fresh and informative, and make sure your readers stick around.

20. ***Go for the Gold.*** Try to get your StumbleUpon page featured on the site. If you get to this level, you'll be amazed at how many more contacts and thumbs up you will get.

21. ***Multimedia Helps -*** integrate video and audio as much as you can.

22. ***Do not Just Link to Other Sites' Home Page -*** Instead, link to specific pages that feature pictures, articles, or other things that are more specific to your topic.

23. ***Mention StumbleUpon in Your Postings -*** True followers of the site really love it, so by mentioning it somehow within your topic, you're making people feel right at home and comfortable.

24. *Create Regular Visitors* - Make sure the people who stumble end up being regular visitors or customers. You can do this by adding an RSS button at the bottom of our page, an email subscription link, or any other method that will bring interested people in even closer.

25. *Be Interesting Without Selling -* In other words, you want the content to sound good and thorough but not like a sales letter or an infomercial.

26. **Stay Away from the Automated Tools if Possible** - since they will end up causing problems in some cases, like creating spam-like postings and will give your pages the overall feel of a robot behind the keyboard instead of a human being.

27. *Make the Content More Social.* Try to achieve a feeling of updating friends and customers instead of a plain informational page. This will make people stay interested and want to know more as things with your business changes.

28. *Edit Your Posts Often* - Have another pair of eyes take a look at them as well. Sometimes, someone else might catch errors or suggest room for improvement that you may not be aware of.

29. *Blog About Your StumbleUpon Page* - Talk about your page on other websites and in other places, so more traffic is led there.

30. *Choose Tags Carefully* - Only use the ones that have the most impact.

31. ***Generate Article Ideas*** - You can generate article ideas and brainstorm concepts by buzzing around the web and finding the hottest topics and other blogs. Take from them as much inspiration as possible.

32. ***Try Not to Use Commas and Apostrophes in Your Title*** - It's been shown to scare people away & indicate to them that the topic will be boring.

33. ***Use the Most Up to Date Tracking Software Possible*** - So you can get an accurate hit count and you'll know how many people have visited the site.

34. ***Visual Impact is Key*** - Make the most of photos, and strive to use the most visually appealing and interesting ones you can that are pertaining to your topics.

35. ***Show Off Some Recent Pages on the Sidebar*** - So people can easily see the other postings you've comprised.

36. ***Capture Emotions*** - Relate your articles to common emotions such as happiness, excitement and even fear to get the point across and garner interest.

37. ***Diversify -*** Don't just stick to one niche topic, but instead broaden your base by writing a number of different things.

38. ***Johnny on the Spot*** - Try to be the first to discover new sites and link to them, so that people consider you a reliable, interesting source.

39. ***Do Not Expect Success to be Overnight*** - Remember that this website takes time to build up a base of people and ratings, so allow it to happen naturally.

117

40. *Make Sure you Comment on Other Peoples' Pages* - and review them as well. This shows you're an active user who cares about what others are saying.

41. *Use StumbleUpon Itself as a Case Study* - to find the best Internet websites out there, and then expand on it by making it even better with new links.

42. *Humor* - really does help with this site, so use it freely.

43. **Keep Your Friends List up to Date** - Only use active members as top friends, so people know you're paying attention to what is going on.

44. *Enable Search Views* - This will help you get more hits in Google and Yahoo!.

45. *Ads* - Watch the number of ads that you incorporate and make sure they're going with the topic at hand. Poorly blended ads can turn people off and confuse them.

46. *Utilize as Many Tools and Tutorials You Can* - There are plenty of great tools and add-ons available, many free of charge, for use with StumbleUpon.

47. *Traffic* - Remember that traffic can last a long time. Even if you gain a lot of stumbles in the beginning and then it dies off, the traffic will still be generated as long as your page is up. Just make sure it's current including your contact information.

48. *Be Exclusive* - Try to feature only certain parts of the bigger picture of your website. This encourages visitors to

actually go there instead.

49. ***Mucho Content*** - Fill up your page with as much content as possible. Some people might skim over the page, some might actually sit and read it all and digest it. More information there is the better.

50. ***Branding is Essential*** - Be sure to have a memorable URL or basic title that people will not forget.

###

"Give a person a fish and you feed them
for a day; teach that person to
use the Internet
and they won't bother you for weeks."

– Author Unknown

Chapter 9

Marketing with Yahoo! Answers

The eighth Social Media opportunity we will explore is Yahoo! Answers. We will once again review, "What is Yahoo! Answers? What are its main marketing applications? And what are the best practices to follow when using Yahoo! Answers?

What is Yahoo! Answers?

Yahoo! Answers is a popular question-and-answer service that's grown to be the #2 reference site on the internet. With such heavy traffic, Yahoo! Answers offers opportunities for some businesses and professionals to gain exposure, improve branding, and acquire web site traffic. And Yahoo! Answers is perfectly fine with using the service to market, so long as users work within the site's guidelines. The site also gives members the chance to earn points as a way to encourage participation in asking and answering questions.

The goal of this chapter was to show you how Yahoo! Answers might be a viable way to increase your exposure and branding as an expert in your field. Yahoo! Answers is a highly-trafficked site that ranks behind only Wikipedia among Internet reference sites. Yes, there's a lot of junk to wade through, but there are opportunities for the savvy professional. When used correctly, Yahoo! Answers can be a source of direct referral traffic, as well as indirect search engine.

Any question is allowed on Yahoo! Answers, except ones that violate the Yahoo! Answers community guidelines. To encourage good answers, helpful participants are occasionally featured on the *Yahoo! 360 blog* page. Though the service itself is free, the content of answers is owned by the respective users — while Yahoo! maintains a non-exclusive royalty-free worldwide right to publish the information. Chat is not allowed.

In order to open an account a user needs a Yahoo! ID, but can use any name as identification on Yahoo! Answers.

Questions are initially open to answers for four days. However, the asker can choose to close the question after a minimum of four hours or extend it for a period of up to eight days. To ask a question one has to have a Yahoo! account with a positive score balance of five points or more.

The points system is weighted to encourage users to answer questions and to limit spam questions. There are also levels (with point thresholds) which give more site access. Aside from this, points and levels have no other value, cannot be traded, and serve only to indicate how active a user has been on the site. A notable downside to the points/level side is that it encourages people to answer questions even when they do not have a suitable answer to give, in order to gain points. Users also receive ten points for contributing the "Best Answer" which is selected by the question's asker or voted on by the community. Unfortunately, some people who answer questions vote for their own answer as the best-- regardless of its actual quality.

The point system encourages users to answer as many questions as they possibly can, up to their daily limit. Once a user shows that they are knowledgeable within a specific category they may receive an orange 'badge' under the name of their avatar naming them a "Top Contributor". The user can then lose this badge if they do not maintain their level and quality of participation. Once a user becomes a "Top Contributor" in any category, the badge appears in all answers, questions, and comments by the user regardless of category.

Points are earned per following Points Table.

Action	Points
Begin participating on Yahoo! Answers	One time. 100
Ask a question	-5
Choose a best answer for your question	3
No Best Answer was selected by voters on your question	Points Returned. 5
Answer a question	2

Deleting an answer	-2
Log in to Yahoo! Answers	Once daily. 1
Vote for a best answer	1
Vote for No best answer	0
Have your answer selected as the best answer	10
Receive a "thumbs-up" rating on a best answer that you wrote (up to 50 thumbs-	1 per "thumbs-up"

Voting and rating with "thumbs-up" or "thumbs-down" is done anonymously, and once done cannot be changed. Users may tag an interesting question with a star, and the list of users who have so tagged a question is made public. On Answers profile pages, users can track how many stars they have received for their questions. However, a user may un-star a question at will. In the event a question is deleted, any stars it had at the time of deletion are still credited to the asker's account. Users may also keep a separate watch list of questions that is kept private.

Yahoo! Answers as a Marketing Tool

Yahoo! Answers is a particularly intriguing marketing tool for use by those selling some form of expertise, such as consultants. Becoming the pinnacle Social Media offering online because of its ease of use and community feel, Yahoo! Answers is a vibrant web neighborhood of information sharing and a fresh alternative to traditional web search.

Audience

Yahoo! Answers is a social network with over *90 million* reported users worldwide and about *18 million users in the United States.* Users appear to be concentrated in the 15-24 and older age groups. Why Use Yahoo! Answers?

Why Use Yahoo! Answers for Marketing?

Providing helpful answers that benefit the community is a great way to brand yourself and attract new visitors to your web site. As suggested above, Yahoo! Answers seems like a natural fit for any business where knowledge and expertise is the main product/service, for example, accountants, investments, engineering services, design, marketing consulting, advertising, new business start ups, and the like are good candidates. Retail businesses are less likely to gain much traction on Yahoo! Answers, although there are some categories in the system where knowledge of certain product types or store operations can be shared.

When you use Yahoo! Answers successfully, it can be a great source of referral traffic, as well as an indirect source of search engine traffic. However, there is not universal agreement on the marketing effectiveness of Yahoo! Answers.

Advocates say Yahoo! Answers can provide a website with significant marketing benefits. It is just important to keep in mind that the primary benefit is going to be highly targeted and trusting traffic. If someone finds an answer to their question on Yahoo! Answers and sees a link to your site as a resource, the level of trust that the user has as they visit your site is likely to be higher than it otherwise would be. This is because your link was used by someone else (theoretically, at least) as a quality resource to address the person's question. Effectively, the resource link serves as a vote of confidence in your site by whoever answered the question.

On the other hand, those who believe Yahoo! Answers to be a waste of time might point to the fact that Yahoo! adds the "no follow" attribute to all of the external links in answers. While this is true, it simply means that your websites will not receive a Page Rank boost from the site. It does not indicate that your site cannot benefit from the links in terms of traffic or by receiving a boost in the other search engines. Digg also no follows links, but very few webmasters will argue that it has no promotional value.

Depending on the topic of your page and the popularity of the related question, you still may receive a hits from Yahoo! Answers.

Tactics & Best Practices

Following are some tactics and best practices which should help you successfully and effectively execute a program on Yahoo! Answers.

1. Become a member of Yahoo! Answers - Upload avatar and fill in your profile with general and accurate information.

2. Identify your Expertise - Pick several topics you consider yourself and your business to be experts on. Do not limit   to just one topic or subject.

3. Select Business Category - Pick the category most relevant to your business or site.

4. *Check that Category Daily* - For questions that you can answer accurately and informatively.

5. *Check Site Daily* - Skim the site daily for keywords that you can jump in and answer in relation to your business.

6. *Links* - Link in your website, Digg site, or other blog related website when you answer questions.

7. *Follow the Rules* -Be sure to read the Terms of Service for the site and make sure you're in compliance.

8. *Think of a Cool User Name* -Come up with a catchy, easy to remember user name so people remember you for future questions and answers.

9. *Ask Questions of Others* - Feel free to ask some questions of your own.

10. *Become an Expert in Your Categories* - Get as much knowledge as possible of the topics you've chose.

11. *Honest Abe* - Be sure your answers are honest and reliable. Do not give false answers just to promote yourself.

12. *Answer Thoroughly* - Do not just answer questions with a word or a link. Be sure to answer it thoroughly first, and then suggest a link at the end.

13. *Be the First Responder* - Do your best to be the first person to answer a question. This is why scouring the site daily is important.

14. *Answer the Right Length* - Keep answers thorough but not too long.

15. *Regional Q&A* - Think about regional questions and answers. This is an excellent way to get new local customers and contacts.

16. *Reference Your Web Site* - Try to incorporate your website in as many answers as you can without sounding too spammy.

17. *Utilize Key Words in Answers* -You can actually use keywords in the answers, so do this with tact and intelligence.

18. *Check Your Spelling and Grammar* - before posting the answer. Mistakes in spelling can be embarrassing and people will question your answers when this happens.

19. *Don't Shoot Yourself in the Foot* - Be polite and do not insinuate that anyone is not intelligent or that they are asking a stupid question.

20. *No Great Pretenders* - If you don't know the answer, do not pretend to. People can smell a liar a mile away, so answer honestly and only the things you know about.

21. *Be Careful of Copyright Infringement.* Do NOT copy and paste answers from Wikipedia if you can avoid it.

22. *Use Language Carefull*y - Avoid slang and emoticons if possible.

23. *This is Not a Chat Room* - Try not to sound as if you're chatting. Instead, use concise, informative language that gives   them a straight answer without all of the filler.

24. Objective - Do not interject your personal opinions, no matter what the question is.

25. Do Not Spam. Do not spam. Do not spam.

26. Videos - You can incorporate videos into your answers, but make sure they are not copyrighted or someone else's videos.

27. Vote - On other peoples' answers and questions, so you are making your presence known.

28. Earn a Top Contributor Badge - Aim to get your Top Contributor Badge on the site. Readers will take your answers a lot seriously if you earn this honor.

29. Stay Away From Politics - Do not answer politically motivated questions unless you're promoting a political website. Otherwise, you could lose potential customers who disagree with your views.

30. Refer People Only to <u>Your</u> Site - Although some answers require a link to other retailers or online stores, as a business it's not a good idea to lead people to anywhere other than your website, or sites that relate to your business niche.

31. Read the Community Guidelines Carefully - on the site before posting any answers on it.

32. Maximize Your Links - You do not have to only link to your website; link to your Twitter, Digg, StumbleUpon, or other page as well, since it will also ultimately lead people back to your contact information and home page

33. Utilize Yahoo Tools - that can help you to scour Yahoo! Answers, and help you use the website effectively.

34. Use Affiliates to Advertise on the Site. Yahoo! Answers has a lot of room for advertising, so see what the rates are to advertise.

35. Use Your Affiliates' Knowledge - You can also recruit your affiliates to participate in answering some questions. This is a great way to recruit more contacts.

36. Beware of Spamming and Over Posting - Yahoo! may ban your account or at least suspend it.

37. Using Key Words - Keyword phrases should be three to five words, and the rest of the content should just be the answer.

38. Research Your Niche - Think about your niche, and then look at the things people are talking about. You can then search Yahoo! Answers for related questions.

39. Ask & Answer - Create a question account in addition to your answers account. answers account. This way, you can be the person asking and answering questions on the site.

40. Perform Searches in Yahoo! for your Top Keywords & Phrases. Answer the questions supplied by Yahoo! Answers in the normal Yahoo! Search results, these will get the most web search eyes and possibly clicks on your links.

41. Make Friends -Use the Yahoo! Answers social network to make friends with every person asking or answering questions within that category. Yahoo! Answers uses a one click Ajax tool for adding friends (contacts) which is very efficient.

42. Be the Answer Man - Answer the questions that you can and link to your site as a reference when best suited.

43. Link to Other Sites as References -so your participation is not mistaken as spamming.

44. Acknowledge Others Better Answers - If others are answering questions more accurately than you, star or vote for their answers, this is a good way to make friends.

45. Manage Weekly - Take two or three hours a week to perform this simple yet effective social media participation, then check your log files or stats to see if this is building traffic and conversions. If it is, rinse and repeat.

46. Consider the Longevity of Your Answers - Take into account that Yahoo! Answers information will be indexed by Yahoo! for a long time, this is not just a quick marketing fix. Yahoo! Answers info is also integrated into Yahoo! Local,Yahoo! Search, Yahoo! Brand Channels and other Yahoo! content channels, so the audience is growing significantly.

47. Promote Only if Relevant - If you think you have a promotional item or contest, etc that will entice people, use hat information in your answers if it is relevant.

48. Use Multiple Accounts - Try not to answer too many questions under one account each day. You can create more than one account at a time so try to switch between them.

49. Answering Your Own Questions - If you do answer your own questions, make sure the writing style and tone is different, or people may notice something seems a bit odd. It's OK to use both accounts as long as it's done properly.

50. HTTP - You must use HTTP protocol links on the site; anchor links do not work.

51. Post Through RSS - New answers to questions can be posted through RSS sign up, so use that for your questions and see what other people are saying. It's a good way to see what the competition or other users are saying.

52. Report Spammers & Trolls - The site depends on its users to point out spammers and trolls, so do your part to report these infractions. You can remain anonymous to the person who is getting reported.

53. Keep Answers Up to Date - As things change, make sure your questions change as well. In other words, current events related or technology related questions might need some updating later on as new information emerges.

54. Report Issues to Yahoo - If you feel as though your answers have been flagged or there are issues, contact the staff at Yahoo! Answers and let them know immediately.

55. Problem – Solution - Try to find questions that ask a solution to a problem, particularly ones that your business or service can fix.

56. *Create Redirects* - You can create a redirect from your link on the site using a PHP code, so look for these codes and implement them into the answer links.

57. *Linking* - Link to others sites besides your own, as long as they lead back to yours in some way, it will be beneficial. many links to your own site is spam.

58. *Don't Go Overboard* - Take a break from time to time, so people do not notice you're posting all day, all over the place.

59. *Do Not Try to Sell Something with Your Answers* - Instead, provide helpful information, and then suggest the links without pushing it.

60. *Learn From Experience* - Figure out what works and what does not and constantly try to develop new strategies with your questions and answers.

###

FREE MARKETING WITH SOCIAL MEDIA

"By creating compelling content,
you can become a celebrity."

--Paul Gillen

Chapter 10
Marketing with YouTube

The last and one of the most important social media opportunities covered in this book is YouTube. Once again we shall ask and attempt to answer, "What exactly is YouTube? What are its main marketing applications? And what are some important tactics and best practices to follow if using YouTube?

What is You Tube?

YouTube is a video sharing web site on which users can view, upload and share videos. Three former Paypal employees created YouTube in February 2005. YouTube began as a venture-funded technology startup, primarily from a $11.5 million investment by Sequoia Capital between November 2005 and April 2006. In November 2006, YouTube, LLC was bought by Google Inc. for

$1.65 billion, and is now operated as a subsidiary of Google. The company uses Adobe Flash Video technology to display a wide variety of user-generated video content, including movie clips, TV clips, and music videos, as well as amateur content such as video blogging and short original videos. Most of the content on YouTube has been uploaded by individuals, although media corporations, including CBS the BBC and other organizations, offer some of their material via the site, as part of the YouTube partnership program.

Unregistered users can watch the videos, while registered users are permitted to upload an unlimited number of videos. Videos that are considered to contain potentially offensive content are available only to registered users over the age of 18. The uploading of videos containing, pornography, and material encouraging criminal conduct is prohibited by YouTube's defamation rule. Accounts of registered users are called *"channels"*

You Tube as a Marketing Tool

YouTube has become an extremely important marketing tool for individuals, companies, organizations, and even politicians. Certain videos go viral and catch the attention of the national press which exponentially increases exposure of the video. YouTube has developed a huge audience and offers an effective communications tool which anybody can use (no doubt to the displeasure of the broadcast television networks).

YouTube Audience

According to data published by internet researcher, *com.score*, Google received about 6.4 billion video views in January 2009--

about 43% of all videos viewed on the internet. YouTube accounts for 99% of Google's video views.

Also, according to You Tube, people are watching hundreds of millions of videos every day on YouTube-- and uploading hundreds of thousands of videos daily. In fact, every minute, ten hours of video are uploaded to YouTube.

Demographically, YouTube's user base is "broad in age range, 18-55, evenly divided between males and females, and spanning all geographic areas. Fifty-one percent of users go to YouTube weekly or more often, and 52 percent of 18-34 year-olds share videos often with friends and colleagues. Commercial Message. "With such a large and diverse user base, YouTube offers something for everyone." (Source. YouTube)

YouTube as an Ad Medium

The Association of National Advertisers (ANA) is extremely concerned about the declining effectiveness of broadcast television, or at least their perceptions of the decline. What is disturbing to broadcasters is the significant decline in expenditures in broadcast television even before the 2009-2010 recession.

Major advertisers are actively looking for more cost effective alternatives which still provide the communications benefits of video-- sight, sound, and motion-- but in a much more targeted manner.

Consequently, more and more companies are using You Tube as a marketing tool where video clips can be hosted for free and people can view the clips for free. The service is so popular that Google recently purchased it for $1.65 billion. In fact some diehard users have stopped watching TV altogether and they prefer spending time watching videos on YouTube. So given its massive popularity, innovative marketers look at it as a perfect opportunity — a free opportunity — to showcase their offerings over there.

Just to give you an idea of the potential media value offered for free on YouTube, some videos have generated over 50 million views. If you bought 50 million impressions on one of the commercial broadcast networks it could cost up to *$1,000,000 or more.*

So, a You Tube video at zero cost can be a great deal!

Another example, the Obama Girl's video (03:18) generated an estimated 3.4 million views, worth around $68,000, plus a huge amount of free publicity in all of the mass media.

It's not very difficult to increase the popularity of your videos over YouTube. The more people who view your video, the higher your popularity grows, and nearer your video goes to the top page, the home page. Once you have uploaded the clip you are given some code that you can use to embed the video into your own blog or website. Even if just 300 people visit your blog everyday there is a probability that 200 will watch the video. You can also increase the views by putting the video link in your email signatures and on all the websites you have.

Then there is a cascading effect. The more people watch it, the higher the video moves, the higher the video moves, more are the views it gets…and so on.

In order to get decent views make sure your video is interesting and worth watching. If you produce a lousy video it could adversely affect your marketing efforts and people may start relating you with the bad video they watch. And also be careful about the copyright violations you may inadvertently commit. Produce your own videos, don't record them from.

Making Videos

Just by using a garden variety video camera you can create small clips and then upload them to YouTube. If you can edit your video, you can also embed your URL somewhere unobtrusively in the video. Of course, higher end video cameras, lighting, sound, and editing equipment would be worthwhile for serious film makers. Just remember that, regardless of equipment, ***content is king.***

It is interesting that the National Association of Broadcasters (NAB) in 2009 talked about TV Production in the Age of YouTube. "Lo-Fi, Hi-Style is about making beautiful content with low-cost gear. In the end it's not the equipment ..." In other words, the idea is far more important than how elaborate the production is.

YouTube.com is not too complicated to use. In fact, the opposite is true. YouTube.com is easy to master. The website allows just about anyone to sign up for an account, upload, share video clips, and view other people's video clips.

YouTubers and potential YouTubers would be advised to steal some of the production planning disciplines from large advertisers who have video production down to a science. For example:

- Determine the length you want the video to be.

- Develop an integrated video and audio script (write it down!)

- Plan out a second by second "storyboard" for the video, showing what the audio and video is supposed to be by second.

- Use the "storyboard" as a template to produce the video.

On the cautionary front, there are some no-no's, which if avoided, could get you into legal trouble. For example:

- Do not upload any TV shows, music videos, music concerts or commercials without permission unless they consist entirely of content you created yourself. The Copyright Tips page and the Community Guidelines can help you determine whether your video infringes someone else's 135 copyright.

- Despite this advice, there are still many unauthorized clips from television shows, films and music videos on YouTube. YouTube does not view videos before they are posted online, and it is left to copyright holders to issue a takedown notice under the terms of the Digital Millennium Copyright Act.

No Videos Required Option

Don't have a video? Don't want to make one? No problem.

If the thought of producing and airing a decent video on YouTube is scary or intimidating, there is good news-- you don't have to produce your own videos to get started on YouTube and have an active social experience. You should will likely overcome your apprehension and publish videos that can connect you with your market, but you don't have to start there.

FREE MARKETING WITH SOCIAL MEDIA

A few things that you can do without producing video content of your own:

- Comment (on others videos, or channels)

- Share (more on that later)

- Create playlists of your favorite YouTube videos

- Rate videos (1-5 stars)

- Favorite videos (another playlist)

1. ***Sharing valuable content.*** For those who are familiar with the various sharing options found on many blogs and social networking sites, you'll be glad to know that YouTube has this function as well. YouTube users can now share a video using one of the popular social networking sites (including Twitter); it also can be sent to one of your YouTube friends, or emailed. YouTube also allows you to embed video content for a single video, a playlist, or a channel.

2. ***Social activities update feeds.*** While not comprehensive as Facebook or other feed activity updates, with the release of *realtime updates*, YouTube seems to be trending in that direction. The fact that this feature has been introduced along with other recent enhancements, there may be other activities will be streamed out as well.

3. ***Understand your video's effectiveness.*** One of the challenges with social media sites is the difficulty in measuring the effectiveness of social media activity. Understanding how the market responds to your content can help video publishers provide relevant content to grow

their business and increase sales. Besides getting feedback from video ratings and user comments, there's Insight Statistics and Data.

4. ***Gain insight.*** YouTube's reporting function helps you understand views, viewer demographics, popularity, and community.

5. ***Community.*** The community tab of Insight reports on how other YouTube users are interacting with your video contents in the form of rating, comments, and favoriting. Used properly, this information can drive future content you publish, making it more relevant and targeted.

6. ***Hot Spots.*** The Hot Spots feature is available on a per video basis, and helps you understand the attention your video has at any point, compared to videos of similar length. Learn where you are loosing interest, and make appropriate adjustments in future videos.

No other social networking site provides this kind of data for free. Let's hope they continue to build on these useful reporting features!

Website Traffic & Conversion

Active YouTube users generate interest in their profile (Channel) page, and this generates traffic to their website (assuming you are naturally peppering links in your channel and video descriptions).

While According to one YouTube user, while "Google remains the number one traffic generator for my site, traffic coming from YouTube users are joining my site for access a special report at 357% the rate of those coming straight from Google search, as the second highest conversion source (Twitter is #1)."

"What this tells me, is that having YouTube as a part of a social marketing strategy is not only valuable, but serves as a very important source of website traffic that converts (opts-in)," he continues.

Tactics & Best Practices

Following are some tactics and best practices which should help you successfully and effectively execute a program on YouTube.

1. ***Viral is the Name of the Game*** - Make the videos viral, and spread them to as many websites as possible.

2. ***Post Videos on Other Sites*** - Use other social media sites like Twitter and Digg to post your videos.

3. ***Video Quality*** - Create well thought out, professional style videos that are edited properly. Just remember that great content with decent video production trumps mediocre content with great video production.

4. ***Sound Quality*** - Make sure the sound on your videos is clear and mixed and edited well so users can clearly hear it.

5. ***Engage the Viewer*** - Keep content funny, engaging, and informative so viewers will watch it from beginning to end.

6. ***Content*** - Try to keep the videos you create clean without too much controversial material. This depends on the purpose of the videos.

7. ***Embed your Logo and Website*** - into the video. You can do this with text at the end or beginning, or by including your logo or URL throughout the entire video.

8. ***Have Goals*** - for your YouTube videos, but remember that there are thousands of videos on the site, and some have millions of hits while others only have a couple hundred. Set realistic goals.

9. ***Good Equipment*** - Make sure you have good camera and editing equipment. If you don't want to sink the money into these things, consider hiring a professional.

10. ***High Resolution Important*** - Keep the resolution of the video as high as possible, so it's as clear as it can be.

11. ***Use of Colors*** - Think about overall color schemes. Some videos may record in a yellow or red hue. This can affect viewer's opinions subliminally, so try to keep the colors realistic.

12. ***Be True to Yourself*** - Do not lose sight of the purpose and mission of the video. Be yourself and loosen up when speaking.

13. ***Most Important is Having Fun*** - Remember that nothing is perfect in online videos unless you have a professional editor, so just have fun and keep the goal in mind.

14. ***Practice Makes (More) Perfect*** - Practice before posting the final video. Do a few dry runs before taping and publishing.

15. ***Consider a Series*** - Create a series of ongoing videos or stories, so users will be hooked and want to learn more.

16. ***Sight, Sound, Motion & Emotion*** - Do more than just talk. People don't want to sit and watch a person just talking to the camera. Make it exciting and interesting as well as fun.

17. ***Ideal Length of Videos*** - Try to limit the video to a couple of minutes if possible. After about two and a half minutes, users generally tend to lose interest and move onto something else.

18. ***Stick to a Schedule*** - if you record a series, otherwise people will just give up on the videos. Be sure to release the next ones on time.

19. ***The Ending is Important*** - Have a sign off that people will remember, then stick to it. This creates a sense of branding.

20. ***Ask for Feedback*** - from your viewers. Some people will not comment unless you ask them to.

21. ***Casting Call*** - Assemble a cast of characters. Use other people in the videos beside yourself. Recruit friends, coworkers, and family members to be actors in the videos.

22. ***Watch Copyright Violations*** - Do not use music on your video that you do not have the rights to. This can lead to all kinds of problems, so either use your own or get permission.

23. ***Title is Vital*** - Do not forget that the title of the video is just as important as the content.

24. ***Key Words in Title*** - Grab viewers by integrating important keywords into the title. This also helps boost the search engine results.

25. ***Use Tags*** - in addition to the keywords, as this also gets peoples' attention.

26. ***Ignore Negative Comments*** - If people pot negative comments, ignore them. By "feeding the trolls" you are encouraging their bad behavior and you might say something you regret later on.

27. ***Embed Video on Other Sites*** - Use as many places as you can to embed your video, like Facebook, MySpace, Digg, Twitter, your home page, and many other places.

28. ***Advance Publicity*** - Let your email subscribers and customers know when a new video is posted.

29. ***Add Communities*** - Add your video to various communities and subject areas of YouTube for more exposure.

30. ***Thank Your Fans*** - Be sure to thank people who post positive comments or consider themselves followers of your videos.

31. ***Be Patient*** - Be aware that not all videos you create will be a hit. It is a hit and miss venture, so be patient and practice making good videos.

32. ***Advance Planning is Important*** - Write the script in advance. While impromptu videos are fun, it's really easy to mess up the vision when you improvise.

33. ***Use Analytics*** - Tools like YouTube Insight to track your sources and hits.

34. ***Actually Use the Word "vVdeo" in Your Title*** - Since people usually include this word, and it will get a lot more results in the search engines.

35. ***Not a Commercial*** - Do not make your video an ad. In other words, get a point across but do it without trying to sell something.

36. ***Choose the Thumbnail Wisely.*** YouTube actually lets users choose their thumbnails so do it carefully and thoughtfully.

37. ***Delete Nasty Comments*** - You can delete comments, so do not hesitate to get rid of negative or rude comments under your video.

38. ***Release Multiple Videos if Desired*** - You can release more than one video at once, so if you have several at a time, feel free to do so.

39. ***Be Real*** - Do not try to fake out your viewers. Most people can spot a fake video or something that isn't sincere.

40. ***Have Fun and Focus on Fun*** so you're creating something people will want to share and forward to others.

41. ***Provide Contact Info*** - Aside from your logo and website, include a way for people to contact you or your business via email.

42. ***Watch Others and Learn.*** By viewing other videos that are

related to your business, you can get a feel for what people are doing, and what others are saying about it.

43. *Stick to Your Target Audience.* Don't try to branch out too far from your purpose, or you could easily lose loyal followers.

44. *Upload Webcam Live Videos.* Have a webcam located at your office, or other location, and then upload this onto your YouTube channel. It's a fun way to get others involved in the day to day operations of what you are doing.

45. *Make a Channel and Profile.* This gives viewers a home base to look at your videos and check on any new ones.

46. *Be Grown Up* - Do not use cuss words or inappropriate language and behavior.

47. *Videos are Show Biz* - Use props, costumes, and other "organic" things in your video. Fancy editing does not always make for the best viewing.

48. *Need a Strong Open!* - Try to open each video with a small montage, song, or your logo, so that people easily recognize your business or who you are. People are most likely to remember the first and last things they see; the middle is remembered less.

49. *Utilize Yahoo! Video* - and other sites to get your video exposed to other audiences.

50. *Specify Your Channel Type* - Have a clear sense of what you're offering on the channel's main page.

Chapter 11
More Social Media Tools

We have discussed nine of the more important FREE social media availabilities-- from Twitter to YouTube, Digg, and Squidoo. However, This book would be incomplete without covering more about blogging and social bookmarketing as important marketing tools..

Blogs & Blogging

Nobody seems to know how many blogs and bloggers there are-- except that there are millions of them-- millions of blogs and bloggers on every subject imaginable—from politics to business and advertising to foods and health to interior design and furniture, aviation, space and science, lawn care, cars and trucks and auto racing, sports, and about anything else you can think of.

What are Blogs Anyway?

"Blog" is an, abbreviation for "weblog," a web-based journal in which people can publish their thoughts and opinions about most anything on the internet. It is everyone's home on the world wide web and probably the number one *venue for venting!*

For example, Burger King might publish a corporate blog to help people understand the nutritional aspects of their products and which are the healthiest from the standpoints of low calories and fat. Or, Political Action Committees (PACs) and special interest groups seeking to influence public opinion generate tons of blogs supporting both conservative and liberal (political) points of view.

Why Blog?

Blogging is the easiest and quickest avenue for non–coders to get their message online. Most blog services are even free for casual or lighter professional uses.

Individuals and companies publish blogs for a variety of reasons mostly having to do with influencing public opinion. Some blogs are launched for marketing purposes, others are posted just for fun or to promote a point of view.

Here are a few things you can do with a *professional blog:*

1. **Free Product Marketing** - Many individuals and companies use blogs for free marketing. Posts can be created as product reviews, articles, news or whatever. You can also link your blog to your corporate or sales sites.

150

2. **Customer Education** - Blogs can be used to inform customers and potential customers. Corporate blogs can contain product news, tips, company news, articles, whitepapers, and more to educate customers or shareholders about products, services or corporate happenings.

3. **News & Information** - Numerous blogs are used to relate current events. Some bloggers publish national news and commentary; others use blogs to cover local events.

What to Look for in a Blog Service

Blogging is usually a highly personal endeavor, so you will want to look for a blog service that meets your desires and needs. Some blog tools are more relevant to personal pages whereas others are integrated with social networking.

On the other hand, some blog services are intended for professional use and include the ability to customize templates, monitor visitors and track referrers.

So when looking for a blog service, pick one that offers you the kind of exposure you want and complements your level of expertise. Below are several criteria you can use to evaluate Blog Services:

1. **Blog Design Tools -** The top blog sites offer an assortment of templates and tools to customize blog entries, including the capability to add photos and sidebar links. Services ought to offer tools for experienced coders as well as non–coders, such as the ability to compose posts in code

or through a text editor.

2. **Promotion/ Tracking Tools-** A number of sites host their own blog site with a directory, other blogging services facilitate blog design and submit your blog to several directories. A few also offer tools to help you track visitors, referrers and comments.

3. **Ease of Use -** Frequently blogs are composed and posted by those that do not code, so it is necessary that the service be simple enough for all levels of expertise.

4. **Technical Help/Support -** Since many blogging sites are free, technical support is principally limited to online documentation like FAQs and a searchable knowledge- base. However, the best sites also post tutorials and a weblog that covers help topics.

***

NOTE: For the easiest to use, free blog service we could find, see WordPress.com. Or if you are interested in working with some simple code, see Blogger (owned by Google)

Marketing Role of Blogs

The growth of using online research prior to buying "considered purchase" products and services services is certainly not a new trend. For years we have seen significant growth in online shopping, but the most notable trend is the emphasis on consumer generated content and how it influences purchasing decisions.

With Universal Search and the emergence of blended search

results, blogs have become even more common and their role has become twofold; marketing and technical. Primarily, blogs provide a forum for *communicating important purchase decision making information* to your customers and allowing them to interact. This opens up communication and provides many consumers with the candid information they are seeking when researching something like automobiles or travel. This is one of the main marketing benefits.

Secondly, blogs provide a *Search Engine Optimization* benefit. By housing fresh content (much of which is consumer generated), you may also benefit from improved visibility in the search engines. Consumer generated content is advantageous technically, as comments provided by your guests provide the fresh content that the search engines view (and rank) favorably

How have you used blogs in your business? How significant a role has blogging played in your marketing efforts? Here is what one business owner had to say about the marketing importance of blogging:

*"**Significant?** Blogs have changed my business completely. When I realized what a powerful tool blogs could be for businesses, I dove in head-first. Patsi and I studied **TypePad** in depth and taught a tele-class for coaches about how to set up a blog. That turned into a blog about blogging (this blog), then it evolved into an ebook, Build a Better Blog, then it became a Tele-Series called Conversations with Experts (Paul Chaney was our very first guest and since then we've done 62 Conversations!). Next came consulting and training and setting up blogs for clients. A whole new business was born and Patsi and I officially became The Blog Squad and business partners, merging our two businesses into one in July 2006, nearly 2 years after we started blogging.*

"Blogs are not my only marketing tool, but a primary one. We have 10+ blogs. Each has a different purpose, whether as a private training system, a private membership blog for clients only, for the public to learn more about blogs, Internet marketing and ezines, or as a way to focus and feature a specific project.

"Blogs have extended the reach of my business in ways I could never imagine. I've met more amazing people through blogging in the past 2 years, than in the prior 8 years of working online. More joint ventures have happened, speaking gigs have materialized, publication opportunities... I could go on and on. Suffice to say, blogs have changed my business AND my life, for the best."

How to Start a Blog - Steps

Anyone can start a blog. It's straight-forward and and FREE.

1. **Select a Blog Provider**

The first step is to find a decent blogging provider that appeals to you. The most popular providers include WordPress.com, Blogger, TypePad, and Xanga as well as others These sites offer pre-made templates and push-button publishing that don't require a lot of technical know-how. Following are examples of three leading providers:

- **Wordpress (****)**
  Promote, inform, amuse or even rant to the far reaches of your brilliance, with WordPress.com. This blog service is fitting for both amateur and prolific bloggers alike and is uncomplicated to use. WordPress.com is a free blogging service inspired by the users of WordPress.org, who requested an easy to use,

154

hosted blog service. WordPress responded by launching WordPress.com. This service is simple, hosts your blog, submits your blog to the Goggle blog directory and monitors your stats; in essence, this is an all–inclusive free blog package.

Unlike many free blog services, this service does not load your blog with ads and WordPress is all about blogging, they are not trying to double as a social networking site. This service gives you every tool you need to build and promote your blog; additionally, WordPress.com is the only free service we found that gives you referrer stats without having to add a third–party application.

- **TypePad (***1/2)**

  Watch your stats, promote your blog and make money with TypePad at less than $5 per month for the basic membership. TypePad offers advanced tools like statistics, word banning, text file uploads and you can publish an *About page.*

  Typepad is a good tool for bloggers who are looking for exposure; this service can also submit your blog to Google, Technorati, FeedBurner and more. If you want to keep your blog private they also support private and password protected blogs. Unlike many free blogs, TypePad does not put ads on your site unless you request them.

  This service is comparable to WordPress, but doesn't obtain the number one spot, because it is not free and they offer few customization features without upgrading to their Pro package.

- **Blogger (***)**

Get the word out with Blogger. Share your life, your product or your ideas for free with this blog service. Blogger has given the world a voice and offers endless template configurations. Blogger launched in 1999, was bought by Google in 2002 and is one of the most popular free blog services. Since they are owned by Google, they make it easy to sign up for Google Adsense and they automatically submit your blog to the Google blog directory so your blog is available to millions.

We liked Blogger because it is easy to use, yet is flexible enough for advanced users who want to build their own templates. The only drawback to Blogger is that you have to add your own traffic tracking devices if your want to monitor your visitors.

2. Choose a Design Template

Once you sign up, you'll have a gallery of ready-made templates to choose from. With these, you can pick a color scheme and layout for your blog. Most sites come with a set of predefined layouts and schemes that you can choose from. Select one and personalize it. Then add your name, interests, images, etc. If you want to, get a more unique template, there are some sites up that have many of these that might make it look better. For example, PimpMyProfile.com or Pyzam.com.

3. Customize

Add blogging freebies like buttons, images, blog chalks, imoods, tagboards (for example, myshoutbox.com), guest maps, guestbooks, comment boxes for readers' input, etc.

4. Private of Public?

Decide whether you want your blog to be private or public: do

156

you want any Internet visitor to be able to read your blog, or do you just want your friends and family to be able to read it? Most blog sites offer the ability to password-protect your published posts so only those who you approve of can view what you've written.

5. Test & Improve

After you've set up your blog, write a few posts to test it out, and make any adjustments to the layout or style that you see fit. Like if you just got a new template, you'd check your blog to see if you like it, right? At first, it will seem tough to figure out what to write, but once you get into a routine   of daily blogging, you will find it addictive. Write about your day, your thoughts, events, ideas, fears, pleasures, the news, current affairs, art, or anything you are interested in!

6. Build a Blogging Circle

Visit other blogs to build a blogging circle. Leave comments. In your comments, include your blogging address so they can visit you too. (Note: This will not work if your blog is private.)

7. Build an Audience

Publish your blog by sending the URL to your friends or publish the URL on your websites. Add the URL to posts you make on other blogs. Register URL with search engines.

Tactics & Best Practices

Blogs have reached into the corporate and government sectors as well. What started out as an outlet for teenage expression and grassroots journalism has turned into a lucrative communications tool for small and large businesses alike.

"Corporate Blogging" refers to a company producing or supporting a blog that it uses to accomplish business or marketing objectives. As with anything, there are certain "best practices" to be followed to ensure your company reaps the maximum benefits. These seven tips or guidelines will help make your blog a success.

1. **Be Aware of Legal Issues**
   Blogging can lead to legal problems. Companies should have real concerns about liability, exclusions and limitations, and indemnity. Although there are laws that protect against libel, misappropriations and other injuries suffered as a result of posts on the Web, companies can still be held "vicariously" responsible for statements made by employees that are harmful to others. Since there are so many legal issues surrounding blogs, it is imperative that the site have some sort of disclaimer and limitation of liability.

2. **Know What You're Talking About**
   Senior management should be educated by the corporate communications and legal department about what blogs are and how they might affect business. That way, they can be contributing members of the blog, further improving employee relations. Their support and participation is often what makes a blog more effective. It is imperative that your blog is factual, well reasoned, and credible.

3. **Create Blogging Policies**.
   In any medium where an employee is sharing information, there is the possibility of leaking trade secrets or financial information. Blogging also has a tendency to become personal. A company should have a list of policies regarding blogging to ensure that trade secrets are kept secret and personal lives do

not become public. Policies may include keeping financial information from being posted, as well as severe consequences for anyone using the blog for negative publicity.

4. **Avoid Overt Marketing & Selling**
Making your blog into a blatant marketing campaign is a bad idea. Customers are looking for real answers and honest opinions. They will pick up on insincerity instantly. Use the blog for what it's for, transparency. This is an opportunity to make a real connection with your customers. Don't ruin it by filling it with empty advertising.

5. **Keep It Fresh.**
Blogs are usually judged by their amount of new content. Easy to add on to, they are designed to be updated constantly. To keep your readers coming back, make your content relevant and timely. Don't forget, content can include anything from product releases to job openings, recent news to thoughts from the CEO. It's practically impossible to run out of material.

6. **Reinforce the Company's Core Values.**
Use your blog to reflect your company's inner soul: its mission, goals and direction. A blog is just another medium by which you interact with your customers and employees. It's another part of the brand experience. It should be consistent with the impression the company wants to make.

7. **Encourage Employees to Use Blog**
Create an atmosphere where they are comfortable asserting their opinions and concerns. You'll be surprised how the quietest employees will speak up when given such an opportunity. With all communication, blogging can become negative, so remind employees of the public nature of the blogs and the ramifications for their actions.

8. Update Often

If you update your blog frequently, more people will return on a regular basis to read it. Establishing a reader base will motivate you to write more and in turn more people will read your posts.

9. **Get into a Routine of Blogging**

Make it part of your day. Soon, you will notice things during your day and think, "Hey, I'll blog this.

10. Personalize Your Blog

A pretty blog always catches the eye. Visit blogger.com for ideas; they have a list of their 10 most recently updated blogs..

11. **Circles of Interest are the Essence of Blogging**

and it can start to develop you as an authority in the "blog-o-sphere" on lawns or whatever area of interest you choose.

12. Keep the Posts Interesting

Try to avoid focusing on things that most readers won't find worthwhile (such as "I went to the mall today and saw Kelly.") Write about things you noticed, thoughts you had, and feelings or ideas. Blog about a recent trip to Spain. Write about the chemical explosion during class.

13. Spell Check!

Spell check your writing before posting.

14. Sell Ads on Blog Site (Google Adsense)

Some sites allow you to make money off your blog by using an Amazon Associates ID or by placing Google AdSense advertisements. If popular enough, your blog could start to pay your bills.

15. Don't Get Discouraged
Don't feel bogged down if no one visits your site for the first few months. As with communities this large, it will take some time for your blog to get noticed.

16. Find Blog Aggregators
They will place a link to your site on their web page and/or have a feed running from your blog so that every time you post something, it will show up on the blog aggregator homepage. Also, this can help increase readership.

17. Language Nuances
If you want a broad (international) readership, do not use too many abbreviations or slang terms that might not be easily understood by people who are not from your country/area

18. Report Interesting News
Get interesting news from Yahoo Oddly Enough..., other Yahoo! stories, Crayon.net and other websites that you frequently read.

19. Focus, Focus, Focus!
Blog on a specific subject. You can't please everyone, so target a specific audience and go with it.

20. Pictures Communicate a Thousand Words
Incorporate as many pictures , video and graphics as you can as they will significantly increase the blog and communication of the blog.

21. Expand Your Blogs' Audience
Post your blogs on Technorati which could multiply your audience.

Technorati: The Blogger's Friend

Technorati is an Internet search engine for searching blogs. By June 2008, Technorati indexed 112.8 million blogs and over 250 million pieces of tagged social media.[The name Technorati is a portmanteau of the words technology and literati, which invokes the notion of technological intelligence or intellectualism.

Technorati was founded by Dave Sifry and its headquarters are in San Francisco, California, USA. Tantek Çelik was the site's Chief Technologist.

Technorati uses and contributes to open source software. Technorati has an active software developer community, many of them from open-source culture. Sifry is a major open-source advocate, and was a founder of LinuxCare and later of Wi-Fi access point software developer Sputnik. Technorati includes a public developer's wiki, where developers and contributors collaborate, also various open APIs.

When you post a new article on your blog, when you link to some other blog or some blog links back to you – Technorati is watching and indexing all information about your blog. Technorati does all this automatically. How must you do to benefit from signing in for a technorati account?

1. Claim Your Blog

Claiming you blog entitles you to add and modify your blog listing in Technorati. This is the first step and you need to confirm ownership of your blog. You need to put a little bit of code on your site, ping Technorati and it will verify that it is indeed your blog. And you get your own blog page (our blog)

2. Edit Blog Description

Once you claim your blog, you can configure your blog settings. Set the description to whatever you like. Fill in your target keywords. Tell them what language your blog is about.

3. Tweak Your Profile

All article listings in Technorati have a link to the author of the blog. This link leads to your technorati profile. This displays all your blogs, their tags and lists the top tags you blog about. Create a meaningful profile to show you are a problogger.

4. Add a Photo

Those with a technorati account can add a nice attractive photo of anything they want. In a long list of results for any search term or tag, articles with photos gain prominence, attract the reader and have a higher chance of getting clicked and drive free traffic to your site.

5. Add the Right Tags

How do you find blogs that frequently write about the subjects you care about? Add your tags and get found on the Technorati Blog Finder page. Become a member to add and modify tags. Claiming a blog lets you enable lisiting your blog in Technorati's Blog Finder. Choose the right keywords to drive traffic from Technorati. This is the way to get listed in Blogs about Technology

6. Keep a Watchlist

Members can maintain a watchlist and keep track of your favorite searches. Add some terms or a web page URL to your Watchlist and never miss a single article about your keywords. Get breaking news in the blogosphere as it happens.

7. Track

Track the latest posts from your favorite blogs all in one nice 7. interface. You can easily add blogs by entering URLs, or clicking the star in any search result. A nice alternative to your usual RSS feed newsreader. Add us to Technorati Favorites. Try it, you can always remove it.

8. Display All Your Blogs

The profile page gives you an opportunity to display all the blogs you have claimed. Claim all your blogs and help readers find and subscribe to all your blogs. Let them know your multiblogging talents.

9. Put Technorati on Your Site

Members can put a nice script with a technorati search, their photo, links to technorati profile and a "Blogs that link here link" that shows how many blogs are linking to your site. You can also add the Technorati Favorites widget that shows the last three posts from your favorite blogs, and a handy search box to search your favorite blogs.

10. Blogs by Country

How do you get your blog added to Blogs about Canada (or other countries)? Add the tag Canada in your tag choices and get listed in the Canada blogs. Only members may add a country tag and get listed like this.

Social Bookmarking

Have you ever e-mailed a friend or family member and sent them a link to a website you thought they might find interesting? If so, you have participated in social bookmarking.

Not only can you save your favorite websites and send them to your friends, but you can also look at what other people have found interesting enough to tag. Most social bookmarking sites allow you to browse through the items based on most popular, recently added, or belonging to a certain category like shopping, technology, politics, blogging, news, sports, etc.

You can even search through what people have bookmarked by typing in what you are looking for in the search tool. In fact, social bookmarking sites are being used as intelligent search engines

Social Bookmarking, also provides more content, more credibility, authority and structure-- so that interested people can can access it with ease.

What is Social Bookmarking?

More specifically, Social Bookmarking is a method for Internet users to share, organize, search, and manage bookmarks of web resources. Unlike file sharing, the resources themselves aren't shared, merely bookmarks that reference them.

Descriptions may be added to these bookmarks in the form of metadata, so that other users may understand the content of the resource without first needing to download it for themselves. Such descriptions may be free text comments, votes in favor of or against its quality, or tags that collectively or collaboratively become a folksonomy. Folksonomy is also called social tagging, "the process by which many users add metadata in the form of keywords to shared content".

In a social bookmarking system, users save links to web pages that they want to remember and/or share. These bookmarks are usually public, and can be saved privately, shared only with specified people or groups, shared only inside certain networks, or another combination of public and private domains. The allowed people can usually view these bookmarks chronologically, by category or tags, or via a search engine.

Most social bookmark services encourage users to organize their bookmarks with informal tags instead of the traditional browser-based system of folders, although some services feature categories/folders or a combination of folders and tags. They also enable viewing bookmarks associated with a chosen tag, and include information about the number of users who have bookmarked them. Some social bookmarking services also draw inferences from the relationship of tags to create clusters of tags or bookmarks.

Many social bookmarking services provide web feeds for their lists of bookmarks, including lists organized by tags. This allows subscribers to become aware of new bookmarks as they are saved, shared, and tagged by other users.

Why Social Bookmarking?

Some believe that proper Social Bookmarking isn't an option anymore. The only question is, how should you get started.

- Social bookmarking was the advent of web 2.0 - from engine determined page ranks to human filtered pages.

- Social networking platforms have turned into real time content management systems.

- People have become authorities in different topics and niches based on the content that they share - they are the source of the most recent and relevant information.

- There is a lot of content constantly being created that its difficult to parse through it, let alone see it all. Social bookmarking allows people to give a good vote to content that they like, and a negative vote to content that they dislike. With the net effect, the content gets filtered as either prominent or buried information.

- Interest groups gather around niche based content

Marketing Role of Bookmarking

Is Social Bookmarking an important tool today important in promoting our businesses, our web sites and our blogs? We will be explore the answer to that question while outlining some strategies for managing the ever increasing number of social bookmark sites.

Fifteen years ago there were just a few websites. People didn't need to bookmark them because there weren't too many of them and they were easy to remember.

A few years later, with more websites on more servers, most Internet browsers added a bookmarking feature. That way, you could bookmark those websites that you liked and find them later with little effort.

A couple of years ago, a new concept was born: social bookmarking. It's a service that allows you to bookmark content, share it with the world and get recommendations about content that you might like based on what people with similar interests to yours have bookmarked.

But there's a lot more to it. Communities have been built around social bookmarking. One person posts a link, people comment on it and a whole conversation starts around that topic.

The most important objective when marketing through del.icio.us is to have your content listed on the 'hotlist' or 'popular' pages on the website. If you can achieve this, without spamming the bookmarks, you have the potential to get a lot of traffic in a short amount of time.

There are no hard and fast rules to producing del.icio.us friendly content. However, you will need to appeal to a large enough audience to get people to click through. What you don't want to do is deliberately advertise your business. You must go beyond thinking about sales and actually offer something, information and content, that a visitor can use. Informative or how-to articles, podcasts and videos tend to rank well, as does content with a high entertainment value. But, again, don't entertain for entertainment's sake. You want visitors who visit your site because they value your message, not because they value your funny video

Instead of having algorithms determine the importance of content, we have humans all over the globe filtering it for us, for free. Voting, bringing to the top, burying ill-represented material, spreading popular content, and so on.

In theory, it's like a machine that consists of all the human brains online. In reality, though, there are ways in which game the system to bring their content to the top. In any case, you need to know the ropes inside out in order to tackle this with care. If done properly, this could be the holy grail of Friend Rank that will help you stamp your authority online.

Social Bookmarking Services

What Are the Most Popular Social Bookmarking Services?

1. Delicious (formerly delic.iou.us)

The most popular social benchmarking service is ***delicious.com*** (formerly del.iciou.us). el.icio.us is a social bookmarking site that has rapidly taken off even more in popularity since being purchased by Yahoo. I use del.icio.us probably the most out of all these top picks, particularly to post interesting sites that I've found around the Web. I also subscribe to quite a few del.icio.us tags, such as popular and reference, and I get all the sites tagged these keywords in my RSS reader of choice, Bloglines.

Delicious (formerly del.icio.us, pronounced "delicious") is a social bookmarking web service for storing, sharing, and discovering web bookmarks. The site was founded by Joshua Schachter in 2003 and acquired by Yahoo! in 2005. It has more than five million users and 150 million bookmarked URLs. It is headquartered in Sunnyvale, California.

Delicious uses a non-hierarchical classification system in which users can tag each of their bookmarks with freely chosen index terms (generating a kind of folksonomy). A combined view of everyone's bookmarks with a given tag is available; for instance, the URL "http://delicious.com/tag/wiki" displays all of the most recent links tagged "wiki". Its collective nature makes it possible to view bookmarks added by similar-minded users.

personal shopping lists, real estate directories, job searches, student research papers, etc. This may just sound like a fancy way of saying bookmarks; but the thing about Furl is that you can access it from any computer, which means that your Favorites will go with you. Delicious has a "hotlist" on its home page and "popular" and "recent" pages, which help to make the website a conveyor of internet memes and trends.

Delicious is one of the most popular social bookmarking services. Many features have contributed to this, including the website's simple interface, human-readable URL scheme, a novel domain name, a simple REST-like API, and RSS feeds for web syndication.

Use of Delicious is **free.** The source code of the site is not available, but a user can download his or her own data through the site's API in an XML or JSON format, or export it to a standard Netscape bookmarks format.

All bookmarks posted to Delicious are publicly viewable by default, although users can mark specific bookmarks as private, and imported bookmarks are private by default. The public aspect is emphasized; the site is not focused on storing private ("notshared") bookmark collections. Delicious linkrolls, tagrolls,network badges, RSS feeds, and the site's daily blog posting feature can be used to display bookmarks on weblogs.

2. Digg

Digg is social bookmarking and social networking gone a little crazy due to the fact that anyone can submit a Digg (site), and then anyone can comment on those same Diggs. For me the most interesting feature of Digg has to actually be the comments on the sites and stories, since the Digg community is not shy about letting folks know how they feel about a particular Digg. Primarily focused on geeky, technology-type items.

3. Reddit

Reddit is a social bookmarking Web site that works much like Furl 172 and del.icio.us: you register a username and password, and then start submitting and sharing your bookmarks. Reddit is similar to del.icio.us in that users are encouraged to vote on the links and stories that they feel are deserving of being in the top dog spot: it's kind of a popularity contest, so to speak.

4. Furl

Furl gives users the ability to save copies of any Web page, search within your own personal archive of Web pages, and share what you find. People use Furl to create their own success. Being true to oneself and your network is the only way to go on social media. When the rewards are so high and the penalty for mistakes so severe, why enter this new frontier without being properly educated on how it works?

Benefits of Social Bookmarking

The internet is increasingly becoming the most sophisticated business tool ever - with businesses selling to, communicating with and supporting customers regardless of their locations.

What's astounding about such movements is not just the efficiency and sophistication, but the cost. The costs are close to nothing. But if you're just another person trying to pave his way through Social Bookmarking without the right strategies, then you'll get buried in the sea of content. It takes a leader to lead, and a good strategist to become a leader.

The question isn't why social media. For all intents and purposes, social media is our only media. What we need to ask ourselves is how we are planning to make social media an effective part of our business. And, specifically, how can we use Social Bookmarking as a medium to achieving that

These sites can spike your traffic in a way you never imagined. Websites that typically may have 100-200 unique daily visitors can get more than 10,000 visits in one day when their links make the home page of Digg and StumbleUpon. That being said, there are two things that I want to make clear:

- Most of the content you try to promote through social bookmarking won't get much exposure. You might have to submit 20 pieces of content before one generates 10,000 visitors to your site. But when this happens, it will certainly make all the difference.

- The traffic that comes from these sites converts very poorly. If you get a 0.1% conversion rate, consider yourself very lucky.

- Search Engine Rankings: The audience of many sites is the "geeky kind." Geeky people tend to link a lot to sites they like. Quality links help you get high engine rankings. And of course no explanation is needed to understand how high engine rankings can make you money.

Tactics & Best Practices

Now that you know why to do social bookmarking, let's talk about the how.

1. Do Your Homework First

You fist of all need to understand the social benchmarking communities in order to benefit from them. The very first step to taking advantage of social bookmarking is to spend a few hours on some of the sites mentioned above. Get a feel for the kind of content people in these communities consume, promote and link to. You'll notice a lot of tech-related content, controversial and funny videos, and other crazy stuff. After spending a few hours on these sites, you'll have a pretty good idea of what works here and what doesn't. But before you start thinking, "Never mind, this has nothing to do with my market", keep reading.

2. Use a Great Headline

Spend some time brainstorming about the perfect headline. No matter how great a piece of content is, without a great headline it will never make the home page.

3. Leverage your Network of Friends

You can bookmark your own content, sure. But you won't anywhere with one vote. Ask your friends—both your real friends and your contacts on these social bookmarking sites, to bookmark our content.

3. It's all about Timing

If 50 people bookmark your content in 15 minutes, you have a much better chance of getting exposure than if they do it in 15 days.

4. Don't Spam

Don't create 50 accounts and bookmark your own content 50 times. You'll get your accounts cancelled and could damage your reputation.

5. Use Free Enabler Tools

Some tools like Socializer, Social Media Add-On for Firefox, and OnlyWire allow you to bookmark your content using several social bookmarking services at a time.

6. Make it Easy to Bookmark

If you have a WordPress blog, there are some plugins for this, including Sociable, ShareThis and AddThis.

7. Tag New Sites & Tools

Every new site or tool you find can be tagged through del.icio.us. Catalog resources and to help me keep track of things you have found.

8. Store all the News and Resources You can Find

You can subscribe to the RSS feed if you wish, but also send the bookmarks down to your Twitter account., etc.

9. What about Backlinks?

"I don't recommend posting merely for backlinks. Why?
Because you need to be different. If your information is good, solid, and informative, you'll get backlinks.
Back linking for the sake of backlinks borders on
It's so much easier to build backlinks when your content is taken care of first."

11. Buttons

Also, you shouldn't limit yourself to del.icio.us buttons only. Add buttons for all of the major social bookmarking and networking websites, such as Digg,Reddit, Furl, Magnolia and StumbleUpon. Your goal should be to drive traffic from as many varied sources as possible.

12. Add to "Delicious"

The easiest way to get your content bookmarked on del.icio.us is to embed "add to del.icio.us" buttons on your articles and web pages that may be of community interest. You can also do this within your RSS feeds as well.

###

Killer Headlines

"Couple slain; police suspect homicide."
"Federal agents raid gun shop; find weapons."
"Typhoon rips through cemetery; hundreds dead."
"Fish need water, Fed says"

Source: Newspapers

Chapter 12
Summary & Conclusions

The use of social media by individuals and business organizations is exploding. The winners and losers among the various sites is still up for grabs, and there will undoubtedly be more ideas surfacing in the future.

Purpose

To review, the primary purpose of this book was to introduce readers (who are relatively new to social media marketing) to 1) how and why social media should be considered for a *free or low cost* role in the marketing mix and 2) some tactics and best practices for actually implementing social media marketing programs (remember, the devil is in the details!) In the process of hands-on planning and executing social media programs for your particular situation, you will no doubt identify many other best practices and ideas, including a list of "what works" and "what doesn't work."

Role of Social Media in Marketing

Social media can perform a variety of marketing functions-- ranging from consumer engagement, creating customer relationships, providing market research, setting off an early warning if there are PR issues or problems gaining steam among consumers *to generating higher web site traffic by utlizing many of the opportunities provided by many social media sites.*

Because social media can be viral, a relatively small following can eventually snowball into many thousands or even millions of customer contacts and/or web site visits.

It's Free!

It cannot be emphasized too much that getting involved in social media is essentially FREE (or very low cost if you choose to spend money). You register for free, set up a profile with key words for free, integrate links for free, post pictures and graphics and product information for free. You may wish to buy advertising or promotion to leverage your presence on a social media site which, of course, is not free, but it is not like spending millions of dollars in network television either.

In this book, we reviewed nine of the more important social media opportunities, each of which has unique strengths and weaknesses, including:

- Twitter (consumer, B2B)
- Facebook (consumer, B2B)
- MySpace (mostly consumer)
- LinkedIn (B2B)
- Digg (consumer, B2B)
- StumbleUpon (consumer, B2B)
- Squidoo (consumer, B2B)
- Yahoo! Answers (more B2B)
- YouTube (consumer, B2B)
- Blogs (consumer, B2B)

Strategy vs. Tactics

As a tactic, doing something good with Twitter may be worthwhile. But Twitter in and of itself may not achieve the kind of impact in the marketplace that you desire.

On the other hand, a well thought out integrated strategy utilizing a variety of platforms may provide the desired impact. A social media *strategy* will likely involve the use of multiple social media platforms which address specific objectives (which ones will depend on your target audience and objectives.) For example, if your objectives are oriented to web site traffic for direct sales, your selection of social media platforms will be different than if your objectives are more oriented toward building consumer or customer relationships through conversations on the web.

An Integrated Social Media Strategy

FREE MARKETING WITH SOCIAL MEDIA

It is likely that a strategy which makes the best use of the social media opportunity will utilize not one form of social media, , but several or many forms, in the following list of social media forms and applications:

Category	Social Network
• Video	YouTube
• Blogging	Wordpress, Blogger
• Microblogging	Twitter
• Purely Social	Facebook, MySpace
• Professional	LinkedIn
• Social Bookmarking	Digg, Delicious
• Community for Discovery	StumbleUpon
• Community creates web sites	Squidoo
• Q&A	Yahoo Answers

Readers can refer to individual chapters to review the potential marketing role and tactics/best practices for effective program implementation for each social media network

###

REFERENCES

2020:Marketing Communications LLC, 2009 *Thumbnail Media Planner*

2020:Marketing Communications, LLC, 2010 Thumbnail Media Planner

2020:Marketing Communications LLC, Internet Advertising Primer, 2008

Advertising Research Foundation, Engagement, 2009

Alexa, web site data

Compete.com, audience data

eMarketer, *Marketers Perceptions of Benefits of Social Media*, 2008

Geskey, Ronald D., *David vs. Goliath: Guerrilla Media Buying for Small Business, a New Way to Win*, 2007

Hilburn, Isabella, blog, Social Media, 2008

Kay, Kate, ClickZ

Quantcast.com, audience data

Social Media Tactics

FREE MARKETING WITH SOCIAL MEDIA

Vollmer, Jeffery, Booz Allen Hamilton, *Always On*, 2009

Web Sites

Wikopedia (definitions, backgound & history on social sites)

www.digg.com

www.google.com

www.facebook.com

www.twitter.com

www.stumbleupon.com

www.squidoo.com

www.yahoo.com

www.youtube.com

Appendix

Examples of Homepages
of Social Media Sites

FREE MARKETING WITH SOCIAL MEDIA

TWITTER

FACEBOOK

FREE MARKETING WITH SOCIAL MEDIA

MYSPACE

LINKEDIN

FREE MARKETING WITH SOCIAL MEDIA

DIGG

SQUIDOO

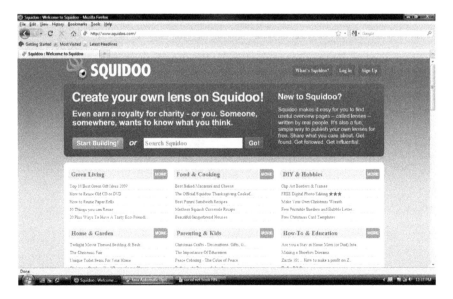

FREE MARKETING WITH SOCIAL MEDIA

YAHOO ANSWERS

YOUTUBE

STUMBLEUPON

WORDPRESS

FREE MARKETING WITH SOCIAL MEDIA

BLOGGER

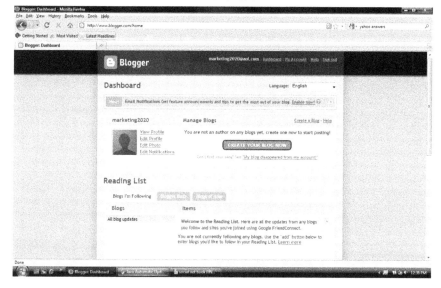

FREE MARKETING WITH SOCIAL MEDIA

Technocrati

Free Marketing: You can get it

in Social Media.

FREE MARKETING WITH SOCIAL MEDIA

2020:Marketing Communications LLC